Simple
Plan for
His Church
– and Your
Place in It

**Second
Edition**

A Manual for House Churches

Nate Krupp

PREPARING
THE WAY
Publishers

*"Making ready a
people for the Lord."*
Luke 1:17

**2121 Barnes Avenue SE
Salem, OR 97306 USA**

2121 Barnes Avenue SE
Salem, OR 97306 USA

Scripture taken from the New American Standard Bible,
Copyright 1960, 1962, 1963, 1968, 1971, 1972, 1973, 1975, 1977,
1987, 1988, the Lockman Foundation. Used by permission.

ISBN 1-929451-12-1
Library of Congress Catalog Card Number 2002-115957

Printed in the United States of America

Dedication

"Render to all what is due them: . . . honor to whom honor is due."

– Romans 13:7

This book is gratefully dedicated to all of those followers of Jesus who have so greatly influenced my life—my parents Paul and Cleo May Krupp; my wife Joanne; and many others too numerous to name, but especially Abraham David, Nate Scharff, Bob Clements, Paul Jackson, Rusty Reynolds, Jim Knutz, Hal Ward, Jim Downing, Jerry Bridges, Howard Noggle, Harold Sheets, Clarence Huffman, Leo Cox, Hubert Mitchell, Ted Hegre, Art Prouty, Maynard Howe, Watchman Nee, Loren Cunningham, Jim and Joy Dawson, Leonard Ravenhill, J. Edwin Orr, Armin Gesswein, Jay Ferris, Jim Watt, and Al Gamble.

About the Author

N ate Krupp grew up in Fostoria, Ohio, in the United States of America. He was converted to Jesus Christ in March, 1957, through the witness of two Messianic Jews during his senior year at Purdue University, where he was Student Body President. He graduated with a Bachelor of Science degree in Mechanical Engineering.

He was discipled by the Navigators while he was an officer in the U.S. Navy Civil Engineer Corps. This was followed by further training with the Navigators, at Marion College (now Indiana Wesleyan University), and with Campus Crusade for Christ.

In 1961, he was married to Joanne Sheets Brannon. They have been together in full-time Christian ministry since then. He conducted personal evangelism training for churches of many denominations, 1961-63, and 1971-76. Nate spent six years (1964-1970) witnessing door-to-door and starting home groups in Chicago.

Nate and Joanne were associated with Youth With A Mission (YWAM) in Hawaii, Oregon, and Washington, from 1977-81 and 1983-86. In this capacity Nate pioneered the School of Church Ministries and ministered in many nations; teaching in YWAM training schools, working with outreach teams, and with local churches. In 1987 he received a Master of Arts degree in Christian Ministries from YWAM's University of the Nations.

The Krupps pastored a church in Salem, Oregon, from 1981-83. Since 1986 they have been serving the Church-at-large. From 1986-91 Nate was calling the Church to prayer—especially 40 Days of Prayer and Five-Day Prayer Gatherings—and to radical change. Joanne began writing a book on God's plan for women.

They were part of the house church movement from 1966-70 and have been working closely with it again since 1987.

Nate is the author of numerous books and booklets on evangelism, prayer, Bible study, and the Church.

The Krupps live in Salem, Oregon. Their two children, Gerry and Beth, are both married and, together with their spouses, are serving the Lord. They each have three children.

Preface

This book has been the combined effort of a large number of people, to whom I am deeply indebted. I first want to thank those who generously provided computers for the writing; Walt and Debi Renfro who gave us their used MacIntosh 512 that I started the first draft on; and George and Joanne Moser who gave a gift for the purchase of a new LC II Mac and laser printer that we used for the refining and final draft. Also, much thanks to Greg Bachran, Tony Dyck, Matt Rawlins, Jeremy Smith, and Lane Witt for helping me learn how to use the computers.

Then I want to thank all of those who diligently read the various manuscript drafts and gave me much helpful input. They include Beth Bachran, Rob Banks, Dave Block, Sterling Borbe, Ritch Carlton, Don and Sue DeBoard, John de Vries, Richard Driggers, Gene Edwards, Jay Ferris, Bob Fitts, Sr., Bob Girard, Jay Grimstead, Rick Joyner, Gerry Krupp, Joanne Krupp, Rosemary Lambert, John Lindell, Dan Mayhew, Rick McIlvaine, Jim Montgomery, Rob and Jean Moule, Hank Niewola, Lindsay Reed, Howard Snyder, Kevin Sutter, Jim Watt, Lane Witt, and Alan Yankus. The final product, of course, is the author's sole responsibility.

There were those whose financial gifts paid our bills and made it possible for me to write.

And there is the one who graciously covered the cost of production. You know who you are!

And it has been a joy to work with Clint and Judy Crittenden of Words Unlimited in the production of the book.

So, you can see, it has been a joint effort. How thankful I am to each of you, and how grateful I am to the Lord for all of you!

The Scripture portions quoted throughout are from the New American Standard Bible unless otherwise noted.

There are many sources which I have gleaned from and referred to; however, that does not mean that I endorse everything which that person or group espouses.

Some have encouraged me to delete certain portions of the book, i.e., my understanding of God's release of women; the ministry of apostles and prophets today; my thoughts on not incorporating and not having a Statement of Faith; etc. They have counseled me that leaving these in will simply make the book more controversial and, therefore, able to be used and recommended by a smaller number of people. I agree! However, I believe the Lord instructed me to include in the book everything that I consider important, that He has taught me, on the whole subject of His plan for His Church.

So I have left it all in. If there is an area you don't agree with, that's okay. Just pass over that section. Don't stumble over that which you can't agree with. I trust that you will be able to use the portions of the book that are helpful to you and simply set the rest aside.

Others have counseled me that much of the book will be offensive to pastors and others in "the organized church." I do not desire to be offensive, divisive, or a stumbling block to anyone in Christ's Church. There is only one Church—His. I desire to bless and fellowship with all who name His Name. And I rejoice over all that God is doing through the existing, traditional church.

However, I believe God has given me a revelation of what He has been after for 2,000 years. And I believe that He has instructed me to make as clear a statement of that revelation as I can. I am attempting to do that in this book. I do not, of course, have any thought that this is the *last word* in God's revelation regarding His Church. All I can do is write what I believe God has revealed to me. I trust that at least some of it will be a blessing to you. I welcome your input if you see where I am contrary to Scripture.

May the Lord build His Church as He wants it—not as I or any other mortal desires it to be. He is Lord! Only He knows best!

Preface to 2nd Edition

The first edition of this book has been used all over the world—by many groups on every continent—as a helpful guide to those who are starting a home church or an encouragement to existing groups. This second edition corrects mistakes, incorporates appropriate changes in the appendices, and reflects a change in the publisher. Otherwise, the basic text is unchanged.

Table of Contents

Introduction

The average person in today's world is *turned off* at the whole idea of *church*. And, increasingly, many believers are beginning to question much of what we do. "Do we really need to invest so much money into these *church* buildings? Is there really suppose to be two groups of Christians: the clergy and the laity? Why does the Church seem to have so little effect upon our society? Why are we not reaching the masses with Jesus' Good News? Why is the Great Commission yet not fulfilled? Is the Church prepared for possible, future, end-time persecution?"

These are questions which a growing number of people are asking—and even more are thinking. This book gives a radical, biblical alternative to today's traditional approach to church; an alternative which may provide answers to these piercing questions. I trust that you will be challenged to consider this biblical alternative to traditional Christianity.

This book is not for everyone. It is very radical. This book outlines God's simple plan for His Church as recorded in the New Testament. It infers that much of what today's church is doing is the *work of man's hands* and is *according to the traditions of men* rather than the Church that Jesus

1

desires. It calls for a complete return to the radical Christianity of the New Testament.

Please allow me to tell you how I have come to these conclusions over thirty-five years of walking with the Lord. I grew up in a small town in northwestern Ohio, USA. There were many "churches" in our town. As a family (Dad, Mom, brother, sister, and I), we "attended church" every Sunday. I am not aware of ever hearing the Gospel preached. Then in March, 1957, while in college, I met Jesus through the witness of two Hebrew Christians! He changed my life! Over the next four years I was affiliated with churches of several denominations in California, Texas, and Colorado.

In 1961, Joanne and I were married and began our full-time ministry of training churches of many denominations for personal evangelism. Wonderful things happened—people were led to the Lord, people caught a vision for lay evangelism, calls were coming for our ministry from all over the United States and beyond. But, six months later, when having contact with these churches, where we had ministered and seen God do so much, everything was back to *normal*—all of the church busyness had snuffed out the evangelism. What was wrong?!

Increasingly I came to the conclusions that it would take New Testament Christians to produce New Testament evangelism, and it would take New Testament churches to produce New Testament Christians. So what is a New Testament Church?

In January, 1966, I was scheduled to conduct several days of personal evangelism training for evangelical pastors from across the eastern U.S. It was to be conducted in Webster, New York, at the invitation of my Free Methodist pastor friend Art Prouty. I arrived a day or two early. A snow storm blew in, and the conference had to be canceled. Art and I had several days on our hands, and we soon discovered that we were both searching for answers: Does God have a plan for His Church? If so, what is it?

Art and I spent those days fasting, praying, and searching the Scriptures together; seeking God for answers. By the end of the time we had reached very radical conclusions: God has a plan for His Church. It is very clearly given in the Scriptures, and it is so non-traditional, that we will probably never see it happen in our lifetime, especially in North America. In the years that have followed, God has used many to continue to confirm, strengthen, and elaborate on what He showed us that week.

So why did God reveal all of this to us? What were we to do with it? Over the years both Art and I have had opportunity to experience various aspects of what God showed us. But not all of it.

In 1986-87, Joanne and I were attending Youth With A Mission's Leadership Training School in Kona, Hawaii, and praying about our future. One day while I was in prayer, the Lord said to me, "Do you remember what I showed you about My Church in 1966?" I said, "Of course!" He said to me, **"Now is the time!"** Wow! What was I to do with this—"now is the time!"?

Since 1987, in our travels across the U.S., we have observed that God is doing incredible things. Many of God's people are looking for

3

something. In many cases, they do not know what it is that they are looking for. Many are leaving the institutional church. They are tired of being an audience, instead of a body. They question increasingly all of the money that goes into buildings. They are tired of being controlled and manipulated. They long to use their giftings to serve God and to see the *priesthood of all believers* instead of the *clergy*. And they long to see the Holy Spirit allowed to freely move instead of everything being controlled.

Instead of *going to church*, many of these people are beginning to gather in their homes to study the Bible, to worship the Lord, to encourage one another, to be involved in one another's lives. **I believe that we are now in the midst of the early days of a sovereign, radical, new move of God!** He is leading His Church back to New Testament Christianity.[1]

This new move of God is being manifested in several ways. One of these manifestations is the growing movement of home meetings which are connected with churches who still meet on Sunday in a traditional *church* building. We rejoice over this trend.

There is another track of this present move of God which includes a growing number of people who question the whole concept of the church building and desire the simplicity of the early Church. It is this latter group who will feel most comfortable with the contents of this writing.

This book has been written to encourage existing house-churches, to give a few guidelines to groups which are getting started, and as a prophetic voice to those in the institutional church who are looking for answers.

This is a very radical book! I would encourage you to ask God whether or not you should read any further. If He says "Yes," please ask Him to give you an open mind and heart. Then read on, dear friend.

I have one great concern as we draw close to the time of the publishing of this book and that is that God's people will focus on the new wine-skin rather than on the Lord. It is true that there is something God is saying and doing today about a new wine-skin. It is a wine-skin which will simply and effectively catch the coming harvest, result in the quick and full maturing of God's people, and be preparation for coming persecution. Much of this book is about this new wine-skin.

But our focus must be Jesus! We must allow Him to be everything in our lives—personally and corporately. We must gather to worship Him. We must live to walk with Him. We must die obeying Him.

Introduction Notes

1. This writer, along with many others, subscribes to the restoration concept of Church history. We find the Church, as God intended it to function, in the pages of the New Testament. It was not a perfect Church, but God's full intentions are outlined there in precept and example. This Church soon began to fall away from God's intentions. By A.D. 500 much of the Church was apostate. The Western world had six hundred years of the Dark Ages. But, beginning in about A.D. 1100, God began to restore His Church to New Testament Christianity. Each century brought new waves of revival and restoration: the Waldenses, the mystics, Wycliffe, Hus, Luther, the other reformers, the Anabaptists, etc. God is still restoring His Church today. When Jesus returns, He will find a Church like we read about in *The Acts*; similar in purity, spiritual authority and power, purpose, principles and patterns, and fruitfulness. We are today beginning to see the final chapters of this restoration. For more on the restoration concept of Church history, you are encouraged to read *Present Day Truths*, by Dick Iverson and Bill Scheidler, Bible Press, 7545 NE Glisan Street, Portland, Oregon 97213; *Root Out of a Dry Ground*, by Charles P. Schmitt, Immanuel's Church, P.O. Box 6598, Silver Springs, Maryland 20906; *The Church Triumphant*, by Nate Krupp; and *The Eternal Church*, by Bill Hamon, Christian International Ministries, P.O. Box 9000, Santa Rosa Beach, Florida 32459-9000.

1 | Does God Have a Plan for His Church?

"See that you make all things according to the pattern which was shown you on the mountain."
                                             –Hebrews 8:5

"Does the Church matter to God? Does God have a plan for His Church? Why is today's Church so different from what we read in the New Testament?" These are questions that most of us have pondered at one time or another.

Most of us have come to the conclusion that God cares greatly for His Church. So greatly that Jesus died for it.[1] God cares so much for His Church that He would not leave its format, planning, and function to mere mortals like us! He cares so much for His Church that He has given us a blueprint for it.

God has given us a plan for His Church. It is found in the New Testament.[2] It is **a plan that is very simple, very natural, and very reproducible.**

God's plan is so simple that we often don't see it. I wonder if the devil has not blinded us from seeing it. It is a plan that will work under any circumstance; it will work in any culture; it will work in any geographical area; it will work in

7

any political climate; it will work both in urban and rural areas; it will work under any economic condition; **it will work anywhere!**

Today, after 2000 years, the Great Commission is still not fulfilled. Every year we spend billions of dollars, are constantly devising new programs, and building new buildings; yet the Great Commission goes unfulfilled. Unfulfilled because, for the most part, we have not followed God's simple plan. **When we return to God's simple plan for His Church, we will see the Great Commission fulfilled, and not before.**

Jesus' Church must be built ". . . *according to the pattern which was shown you on the mountain.*"[3] And we must let Him do the building![4] (More about this in Chapter 2.) So, do we want the Church that men have devised or the one that God has in mind? And, do we want the Church which men can organize or the one that Jesus can build?!

Today, as never before, God is calling His people to return to His simple plan for his Church. The rest of this book is a look at this plan.

Chapter 1 Notes

1. Acts 20:28; Ephesians 5:23-32
2. 2 Timothy 3:16-17. George Patterson, in his book *Church Multiplication Guide*, explains that the New Testament contains (1) commands, (2) apostolic practices, and (3) customs. The commands we must keep, the apostolic practices we will probably desire to do, the customs we may want to steer clear of. For more on these delineations, you may order the book from Church Planting International, P.O. Box 1002, Cucamonga, California 91730.
3. Hebrews 8:5
4. Matthew 16:18

2 | Who is Lord?

"He is also head of the body, the church; and He is the beginning, the first born from the dead; so that He Himself might come to have first place in everything." –Colossians 1:18

God gave His Son to redeem a people—the *ekklesia*, the *called-out ones*, a people called out of the world unto Himself—for His own possession.[1] Jesus did not die to start an organization! He died to redeem a people that He can possess, individually and corporately; an organism; a people that He can live in, own, lead, be glorified by. He did not die for the erecting of a building. He died to provide a house made of living stones—a living, functioning, organism.[2]

Source of Life

To this Church God gave Jesus to be the Head, i.e., the *source of life*.[3] He is the *source of life* for every person.[4] He is nourisher and source of growth to His Church.[5] He is the One Who brings the Church to purity and completion.[6] He is the Originator and Completer of the Church and the Nourisher and Enabler Who brings the Church to fullness of life.[7] He is the source of life for the whole Body.[8]

This Church is to express the fullness of Christ: His love, His joy, His beauty, His compassion, His wisdom, His knowledge, His faithfulness, His grief, His wrath, etc.[9] No human being or man-devised program can produce these attributes. They come from Him alone. He, through the Holy Spirit, is the source of any and all good that flows from His Church.

Jesus died to create the Church, and He lives to give life to it. There is no life in Jesus' Church unless He is there. He has promised to be there, wherever two or three have gathered in His Name.[10] But we need to **believe His promise**, **allow His Holy Spirit to fill us**, consciously **recognize His presence**, and **surrender to His leading** if we are to know the full benefits of Him as the *source of life*.

Governmental Authority

Jesus is also the governmental authority over His Church.[11] The most common Greek word for the English word *authority is exousia,* and means the "liberty of doing as one pleases, the right to exercise power, rule, government, the power of one whose will and commands must be obeyed by others."[12] Jesus is the authority over His Church; He is the governing power; He is the Ruler; He is the One whose will and commands we are to obey.

How easy it is to call Him Lord, but not spend our lives doing His will.[13] All things were created for Him.[14] He is to have first place in everything.[15] The Church is to belong to Jesus and to Him alone—not to any man. **Everything**

---

we do, as individuals and as groups of believers, must be at His command: doing His will—totally, completely, fully, carefully, instantly, joyfully!

Who is Lord—Jesus or Man?

Jesus is Lord. He is the total Source and only Authority over His Church. He wants to lead and give life to every believer and to every group of believers. No organization, no hierarchy, no bishop, **no human is to usurp Jesus' place of being directly in charge of every believer and every group of believers.** Jesus' will can be accomplished only as He is allowed to lead His Church—each person, and each group of believers.[16]

Too much of the Church today, like in Samuel's day, has rejected Jesus' rulership and substituted it with man's.[17] And men love to rule! Too much of the Church today is ruled by men who are influenced by a Nicolaitan spirit of control[18]—men who have to make every decision and be in control of everything that goes on. The Church is Jesus'! Only He can build it![19] No man can build the Church that Jesus desires. All of our humanly-devised schemes and programs are *wood, hay, and straw.*[20] We need to repent of our trying to build His Church. We need to get out of the way and allow Jesus to do the building.

May we repent of all our Babylonian systems of men.[21] Let us return to Jesus.[22] Let us look to Him alone as our source for everything. May we give the Church to Him so that He alone is allowed to lead it. Let's let Jesus build His Church. **Let us allow Him alone to have the first place in everything.**[23] Amen!

Chapter 2 Notes

1. John 3:16; 1 Peter 2:9
2. 1 Peter 2:5; 1 Corinthians 12-14; Ephesians 4:12-16
3. The Greek word for *head* is *kephale*. Traditionally it has been understood to be speaking of governmental authority. More recent scholarship, however, seems to conclude that *kephale* means *source of life*. This can be verified by checking the most complete Greek-English lexicon available: Henry George Liddell and Robert Scott, *A Greek-English Lexicon*, revised by Henry Stuart Jones, with the assistance of Roderick McKenzie (Oxford: Clarendon Press, 1940), 1:944-45. An excellent study of the word *kephale* is also found in *Women, Authority & the Bible*, edited by Alvera Mickelsen, InterVarsity Press, Downers Grove, Illinois 60515, 1986, pp. 97-132. Also see *Does* Kephale *Mean* Source *or* Authority Over *in Greek Literature?: A Rebuttal*, by Richard S. Cervin, available from Christians for Biblical Equality, St. Paul, Minnesota 55107, a 19 p. paper; *Beyond Sex Roles*, by Gilbert Bilezikian, Baker Book House, Grand Rapids, Michigan 49516, 1985, pp. 215-52; and *Church Leadership*, by Lawrence O. Richards and Clyde Hoeldtke, Zondervan, Grand Rapids, Michigan 40506, 1980, pp. 14-28. Jesus is our *source of life*.
4. 1 Corinthians 11:3
5. Ephesians 4:15
6. Ephesians 5:23-27
7. Colossians 1:18, 2:9-10
8. Colossians 2:19
9. Ephesians 1:23
10. Matthew 18:20

11. Matthew 18:18; 1 Corinthians 15:24; Colossians 2:10; Jude 25; Revelation 12:10

12. *Vine's Expository Dictionary of Old and New Testament Words*, Fleming H. Revell, Old Tappan, New Jersey, 1981, p. 89.

13. Matthew 7:13-27

14. Colossians 1:16

15. Colossians 1:18

16. There is a place for the overseeing guidance and protection of elders (we will look at this in Chapter 12). And there is a place for apostolic and prophetic input (we will look at this in Chapter 13). But Jesus alone is to be in charge of His Church.

17. 1 Samuel 8:7

18. The term *Nicolaitans* is found in Revelation 2:6 and 2:15. The *Scofield Reference Bible*, Oxford University Press, New York, NY, 1945, p. 1332, has the following explanatory note: "From *nikao* (to conquer), and *laos* (the people), or *laity*. There is no ancient authority for a sect of the Nicolaitanes. If the word is symbolic, it refers to the earliest form of the notion of a priestly order or *clergy*, which later divided an equal brotherhood (Matthew 23:8) into priests and laity. What in Ephesus was *deeds* (Revelation 2:6) had become a *doctrine* in Pergamum (2:15). Not all authorities agree with this view. (Scofield changed this note in later editions because of pressure he was receiving from many church leaders!)

19. Matthew 16:18

20. 1 Corinthians 3:10-15

21. Revelation 18:2-5

22. Revelation 2:4-5, 3:14-22

23. Colossians 1:18

3 | The *Ekklesia*

"But you are a chosen race, a royal priesthood, a holy nation, a people for God's own possession, that you may proclaim the excellencies of Him who has called you out of darkness into His marvelous light." —1 Peter 2:9

The English word *church* is the way most translations of the English Bible render the Greek word *ekklesia.* This Greek word occurs 114 times in the New Testament.[1] Twice it is translated *congregation* and refers to an assembly of the Children of Israel.[2] Three times it is translated *assembly* and is referring to groups of people other than Christians who are assembled together.[3] The remaining 109 times it is translated *church* or *churches.*

This word *ekklesia* is translated into English as the *called out ones*[4]—those who have been called out of the world into a relationship with the Father through the atoning death of His Son by the working of the Holy Spirit. It is talking about people. It never means a building. It never refers to a denomination. It is never used referring to an organization. Only people!

We are the church! We don't *go to church.* We don't *join the church.* We don't *have church.* **We**

are the church. Until God gives you a heart revelation of this truth, nothing else in this book will make any sense.

Jesus did not die for buildings! Jesus did not die to create corporate organizations called *churches.* Jesus did not die to create denominations. He died to call out of the world a people for Himself—a people who would be in loving, right relationship with Himself and loving, right relationships with each other.[5] **Jesus died to create an organism—a world-wide, living, functioning Body of people—rightly related to Him and to each other.**

The ekklesia, the called-out ones, **people**— that's the church. Nothing more, nothing less.

Chapter 3 Notes

1. In the New American Standard Bible.
2. Acts 7:38; Hebrews 2:12
3. Acts 19:32, 39, and 41
4. The Greek word *ekklesia* is a composite of the Greek word *ek* which means *out of*, and *klesis*, a derivative of *kaleo* which means *called*. Thus, *ekklesia* has a meaning of *ones called out of* or, more simply, the *called out ones*. *Greek Dictionary of the New American Standard Exhaustive Concordance*, Holman Publishers, Nashville, Tennessee, 1981, no. 1577; and *Vine's Expository Dictionary of New Testament Words*, Fleming H. Revell, Old Tappan, New Jersey, 1981, pp. 83-84.
5. Ephesians 2

4 | God's Great Salvation

"... I came that they might have life, and might have it abundantly." —John 10:10

The Church is people, i.e., the *called out ones*, the people who have been called out of the world into God's great salvation. The word *salvation* comes from the Greek word *soteria* which can be translated *salvation, deliverance, soundness, wholeness.*[1] God's desire in saving a people unto Himself is to deliver them from sin, spiritual death, and hell, and bring them into a *wholeness* in all of life. He wants to make us whole spiritually, mentally, emotionally, and physically. Let's take a look at the various aspects of God's great salvation.

The New Birth

The first aspect of God's great salvation is the new birth.[2] The new birth is preceded by a process of being awakened and convicted. First, the Holy Spirit begins to awaken a person to their need for salvation and convict them of their life of sin and godlessness.[3] As one begins to respond to the Holy Spirit's dealings, he will begin to be sorry for, and want to turn from, his sins.[4]

He will turn from his sins, put his faith in the blood of the Lord Jesus Christ as the only and full payment for his sins,[5] and turn to Him as his only Savior and Lord.[6] As one does this, turns from sin and turns to the Savior, he experiences the *new birth*.[7] God's Spirit comes to reside in him.[8] God adopts him into His family as His child.[9] He becomes part of Christ's body, the *ekklesia*.[10] His life begins to change from one of serving self, sin, and the Law, to one of serving Jesus.[11]

Water Baptism

The step one takes to demonstrate that he is turning from his sin and turning to Jesus as Savior and Lord is to be baptized in water.[12] As you prayerfully study the various passages on the subject of water baptism found throughout the New Testament, you will come to your own understanding as to its full significance and how it is to be administered (more on water baptism in Chapter 19).

Baptism in the Holy Spirit

In addition to being *born of the Spirit*, there is also the Holy Spirit's ministry of *baptizing* or *filling* the believer. The Bible says that Jesus would baptize people with the Holy Spirit.[13] This Spirit baptism is an enduement with power for service. It includes a purifying dimension, i.e., *fire*.[14] We find this *enduement with power* mentioned a number of places in the New Testament.[15]

Various terminology is used with reference to this experience: the *baptism of* (or *in*) *the Holy*

Spirit;[16] being *filled with the Spirit;*[17] *receiving the Spirit;*[18] being *endued* (or *clothed*) *with power from on high;*[19] the Holy Spirit *falling* or *coming upon;*[20] the *gift of the Holy Spirit;*[21] the *promise of the Father;*[22] and the Holy Spirit being *poured out.*[23]

Many of God's great servants, including John Wesley, Charles Finney, George Mueller, D.L. Moody, R.A. Torrey, Hudson Taylor, Billy Graham, and Oral Roberts, have testified to, and taught, a definite time after conversion when they were baptized, or filled, with God's Holy Spirit.

You are encouraged to seek God for the *baptism in the Holy Spirit.* You may also want to ask others who have already experienced it to pray with you and lay their hands upon you.[24]

Deliverance from Demon Activity

Jesus spent much of His time casting demons out of people.[25] Many of us, when we come to the Lord, have areas of our lives where demons have control. These demonic strongholds need to be broken and the demons cast out. This is all part of God's great salvation, bringing us to wholeness.[26]

Healing

Jesus also spent much of His time healing people.[27] He told His disciples to heal.[28] He said healing would be part of the Gospel for the entire Church Age.[29] We find the apostles and others healing the sick in *The Acts.*[30] Healing is part of what Jesus died to provide.[31]

This healing is for the total person: body, mind, emotions, and spirit.[32] Some Scriptures which refer to mental, emotional, and spiritual healing include:

Psalm 147:3 – "He heals the brokenhearted."

Isaiah 53:4 – "Our griefs He Himself bore, and our sorrows He carried."

Isaiah 61:1 – "He has sent me to bind up the brokenhearted."

Jeremiah 30:17 – "I will heal you of your wounds."

Ephesians 4:23 – "Be renewed in the spirit of your mind."

In Conclusion

Let's enter into God's great salvation. Let's not stop short of His wholeness. Thank God for the new birth, but let's also move on to water baptism, the baptism in the Holy spirit, deliverance, healing, and wholeness for the total person. And let's pray for the sick, the demon afflicted, and the brokenhearted, and believe God to heal them and set them free. God wants His *ekklesia* to be an army of whole people!

Chapter 4 Notes

1. *Thayer's Greek-English Lexicon of the New Testament*, Baker Book House, Grand Rapids, Michigan, 1977, pp. 612-613; and *Vine's Expository Dictionary of Old and New Testament Words*, Fleming H. Revell, Old Tappan, New Jersey, 1981, pp. 316-317.

2. John 3:3-16

3. Psalm 38:4; John 16:7-11; Acts 2:37, 16:29-30, 24:25; 2 Corinthians 7:10

4. Psalm 34:18, 51:17; Ezekiel 18:31; Joel 2:12-13; Matthew 3:2; Luke 3:3; Acts 3:19, 17:30, 26:20; 2 Corinthians 7:10. The word *repent* means to *be sorry for, and turn away from, one's sins.* See *Thayer's*, pp. 405-06; and *Vine's*, pp. 279-81.

5. John 3:16-18; Romans 1-5; 1 Peter 1:18-19

6. Acts 3:19, 20:21

7. Ezekiel 36:26; John 1:12-13, 3:3-16, 6:63; 2 Corinthians 3:6; Titus 3:5; 1 Peter 1:23; 1 John 5:1

8. Romans 8:9-17

9. John 1:12; Romans 8:14-17; Galatians 3:26, 4:4-8

10. 1 Corinthians 12:12-13

11. Romans 6-8; 2 Corinthians 5:17; entire book of Galatians

12. Matthew 28:19-20; Mark 16:15-16; Acts 2:37-41, 8:36-39, 9:18, 10:48, 16:30-34; Romans 6:1-11

13. Matthew 3:11; Mark 1:8; Luke 3:16; John 1:33

14. Matthew 3:11-12; Luke 3:16-17

15. Matthew 3:11; Luke 24:49; Acts 1:8, 2:4, 33, 4:8, 31, 6:8, 8:17, 9:17, 10:44-47, 19:2-6; Galatians 3:14

16. Matthew 3:11; Acts 1:5, 11:16

17. Acts 7:4, 4:8, 31; 9:17

18. Acts 8:15, 17; 10:47, 19:2

19. Luke 24:49
20. Acts 1:8, 8:16, 10:44, 11:15, 19:2
21. Luke 11:13; Acts 2:38, 10:45, 15:8
22. Luke 24:49; Acts 1:4, 2:33
23. Acts 2:17, 33; 10:45
24. Acts 8:15-17, 19:6
25. Matthew 9:32-34; Mark 1:21-28, 7:24-30, 9:14-29; Luke 8:26-39, 13:10-17, 31-32
26. For additional reading on the subject of deliverance from demonic activity, we recommend *Demons & Deliverance in the Ministry of Jesus* by Frank Hammond, The Children's Bread Ministry, P.O. Box 789, Plainview, Texas 79073; *Handbook on Deliverance* by Russell J. Meade, Creation House Publishers, 499 Gundersen Drive, Carol Stream, Illinois 60187; *Strongman's His Name. . . What's His Game?* by Carol & Jerry Robeson, Shiloh Publishing House, P.O. Box 100, Woodburn, Oregon 97071; *The Three Battlegrounds* by Francis Frangipane, Advancing Church Publications, P.O. Box 46, Marion, Iowa 52302; and *War on the Saints* by Jessie Penn-Lewis with Evan Roberts, Thomas E. Lowe, Ltd., P.O. Box 1049, Cathedral Station, New York, NY 10025.
27. Matthew 4:24, 8:13, 16, 12:15, 22, 14:14, 15:28, 30, 19:2, 21:14
28. Luke 9:1-2, 10:9
29. Mark 16:18
30. Acts 3:6-8, 5:12-16, 8:7, 9:32-34, 28:8
31. Matthew 8:17; Isaiah 53:4-5; 1 Peter 2:24; James 5:14-18
32. For additional books on healing, we recommend *Christ the Healer* by F.F. Bosworth, Revell, Old Tappan, New Jersey; *Healing the Sick*

by T.L. Osborn, Harrison House, P.O. Box 35035, Tulsa, Oklahoma 74153; *Healing the Wounded Spirit* by John and Paula Sandford, Bridge Publishing, South Plainfield, New Jersey; *How to Heal the Sick* by Charles and Frances Hunter, Hunter Books, Kingwood, Texas 77339; and *The Search for Significance* by Robert S. McGee, Rapha Publishing, 8876 Gulf Freeway, Houston, Texas 77017.

5 | Walking with God

"As you therefore have received Christ Jesus the Lord, so walk in Him." —Colossians 2:6

For too long we have taught people to *go to church* instead of to *walk with God*. God's people, the *ekklesia*, who have entered into His great salvation, need to learn to walk with God. We would offer a few suggestions.

Walk in Humility

You entered Christ's Kingdom by humbling yourself, seeing your need for God, turning from your sin, and turning to Him. You will continue to walk with Him by continuing to live a life of humility, repentance, brokenness, and death to self.[1]

Walk in Trust

You were received into God's family by trusting in God's faithfulness and Jesus' blood. You need to continue to trust in the blood of Jesus to keep you clean from all sin.[2] And you need to continue to live a life of continuous trust in God's moment-by-moment faithfulness to you in every detail of life.[3]

Walk in Full Surrender

Romans 12:1 says, "*I beseech, urge, and appeal to you, brothers and sisters, because of God's overwhelming compassion and mercies, that you make a full and decisive surrender and dedication of your whole being and life, as a sacrifice to God, because that's the only reasonable thing to do*" (author's paraphrased translation). If you have never done this—"*make a full and decisive surrender and dedication of your whole being and life*" to God—you need to do it NOW! Give everything to Him—your time, talents, weaknesses, assets—your total being and your whole life—for Him to do with as He chooses. Then, and only then, is He free to fully mold you, lead you, bless you, and make of your life what He would choose for His own glory.

Walk in Obedience

We have entered a relationship with God through Jesus Christ. It is to be a life spent doing His will, joyfully obeying Him.[4] John 15:1-10 talks of the life of abiding in Christ. Various New Testament translations render *abiding* as *remaining in, dwelling in, continuing in, staying joined to, staying united to, remaining in union with, living in,* and *maintaining a living communion with.* This is a life of obedience to Him. As Jesus says in John 15:10,

> If you keep My commandments, you will abide in My love; just as I have kept My Father's commandments, and abide in His love.

30

Walk with a Blameless Conscience

In Acts 24:16, Paul says, *"I also do my best to maintain always a blameless conscience before God and before men."* This should be a constant goal for each of us. We need to have a conscience always clear before God. If we do anything contrary to God's will, and the Holy Spirit shows that to us, we need to immediately repent of that sin, ask God's forgiveness, and be freshly cleansed by Jesus' blood.[5]

Likewise, in our relationship with people, we are to have a clear conscience toward all. Romans 12:18 says, *"If possible, so far as it depends on you, be at peace with all men."* Sometimes it is not possible; some people make it very difficult for us to walk with them. But we should do everything we can to have a clear conscience toward all. Once again, if the Holy Spirit shows you that you have offended someone, you need to go to that person as soon as possible and ask their forgiveness. This means being open and transparent in our relationships.

Walk in the Word

Jesus said we are to live by *"every word that proceeds out of the mouth of God"* (Matthew 4:4). 2 Timothy 3:16-17 says that the Scriptures give us everything we need to live an exciting life that is pleasing to God. Psalm 19:7-11 and Psalm 119 tell us much about the benefits of God's Word in our lives.

We should spend as much time in God's Word daily as we can:

- reading it (Deuteronomy 17:18-20; 1 Timothy 4:13; Revelation 1:3)

- studying it (Proverbs 2:1-5; Ezra 7:10; Acts 17:11; 2 Timothy 2:15)

- memorizing it (Deuteronomy 11:18; Psalm 119:11; Proverbs 7:1-3; 1 John 2:14)

- meditating upon it (Joshua 1:8; Psalm 1:1-3)

- obeying it (Matthew 4:4, 7:13-27; John 14:21, 23; James 1:22-24; 1 John 1:7)

- passing it on to others (Ezra 7:10; 2 Timothy 2:2)

Set aside time just for you and God's Word. Many find the first part of the day to be best.[6] Begin by taking just fifteen minutes to read one chapter. Begin with John's Gospel or First Epistle. Ask God to speak to you through His Word.[7] Before long you will be getting up early and spending an hour in God's Word to begin your day and will be launching on a schedule of Bible reading, study, memory, and meditation. And with Jeremiah you will say, *"Thy words became for me a joy and the delight of my heart"* (Jeremiah 15:16).

As we continue to search God's Word, our purpose should not be to just gather more information, but to go deeper in our knowledge of God and His ways,[8] and to become more like Him.[9]

Walk in Prayer

The life of the follower of Jesus should be characterized by much prayer.[10] Various aspects of prayer include:

- waiting upon God (Psalm 25:5, 21, 27:14, 37:7, 9, 34, 52:9, 62:5, 69:3, 6, 130:5, 147:11)

- adoring and worshiping God for Who He is (Exodus 24:1; Psalm 8; Revelation 4-5)

- confessing our sin (Psalm 51; 1 John 1:9)

- thanksgiving and praise for His acts of kindness and blessing (1 Thessalonians 5:16-18; Psalm 148)

- supplication, praying for one's own needs (1 Samuel 1:10-11; Acts 4:29-30)

- intercession, praying for the needs of others (Exodus 32:10-14)

- warfare, praying against the devil and his forces (Mark 3:27; Ephesians 6:12)

So, begin your day looking to Him in prayer. Set aside time just for prayer. Many find the first thing in the morning to be the best time. Begin to practice His presence and look to Him in prayer as you go throughout the day. You will soon find that you are in conscious communication with Him almost every moment of the day. What a privilege—to be in instant and constant communication with the Creator of the universe and your Lord and Savior!

Walk in the Spirit

After having experienced the baptism in the Holy Spirit (see Chapter 4), one needs to learn to walk in the Spirit, i.e., to be led moment-by-moment by God's Holy Spirit.[11] In Acts 8:29 we see the Holy Spirit telling Philip to go and become a passenger in the eunuch's chariot. In

Acts 16:6-7, the Holy Spirit forbids Paul, Silas, and Timothy from going into Asia and Bithynia. What a wonderful life, being led by God's Holy Spirit, being directed each day where to go, where not to go, what to do, and what to say! This is walking with God!

In Conclusion

Romans 14:17 tells us that God's Kingdom in our lives is characterized by righteousness, peace, and joy. This is the life of walking with God—a life of repentance, humility, brokenness, death to self, trust in God, full surrender, obedience, a blameless conscience, God's Word, prayer, and being led by the Holy Spirit. And this life of walking with God results in righteousness, joy, and peace. What a life—walking with God!

Chapter 5 Notes

1. Matthew 5:3-12, 18:4; John 12:24; Romans 12:16; Philippians 2:5-8
2. 1 John 1:7
3. Lamentations 3:21-23; Matthew 6:25-34
4. Matthew 5:19, 6:24, 7:13-27, 12:50; Luke 11:28; John 3:36, 14:15, 21, 23-24; Acts 5:29; Romans 6:16-19; Philippians 2:12-13; 1 John 2:3-6, 2:17, 3:22-24, 5:2-3
5. 1 John 1:6-9
6. Genesis 28:18; 2 Chronicles 29:20; Job 1:5; Psalm 57:8; Mark 1:35
7. Psalm 119:18
8. Exodus 33:13; Deuteronomy 8:6; Joshua 22:5; Psalm 25:4
9. Romans 8:29
10. 1 Thessalonians 5:17
11. Romans 8:14; Galatians 5:16-18, 5:25

6 | The Church Gathered

"What is the outcome then, brethren? When you assemble, each one has a psalm, has a teaching, has a revelation, has a tongue, has an interpretation. Let all things be done for edification." —1 Corinthians 14:26

The Importance of Gathering Together

In the previous chapters, we considered God's people, the *ekklesia*, experiencing God's great salvation and walking with Him. Now what? This *ekklesia*, the *called out ones*, the *church*, is to function in two settings. There is the *church gathered*, when the saints come together, and there is the *church scattered*, when the church is scattered throughout the world—in our neighborhoods, our places of employment, and the market place. This chapter deals with the *church gathered*. The next chapter deals with the *church scattered*.

One of God's great desires for His Church is that she come together. As we have already noted in Chapter 3, the most basic meaning of the Greek word *ekklesia* is the *called out ones*. But a secondary meaning is *called to assemble* as used in Acts 19:39 referring to an assembly of citizens, Acts 7:38 referring to an assembly of Israel, and

Acts 19:32 and 19:41 referring to an assembled mob.

Many Scriptures refer to the church being gathered together: Acts 20:7 talks of the church *gathering together*; Hebrews 10:24-25 talks of the church *assembling together*; 1 Corinthians 14:26 states *when you assemble*; 1 Corinthians 11:17-18 has *come together*; and 1 Corinthians 11:20 says *meet together*.

With Whom Should You Gather?

Only one criterion answers that question: those with whom God links you. There is such a thing as God-formed relationships; people with whom God bonds you. These God-ordained and God-formed relationships are very important. God's purposes for you and for His Kingdom will come to pass as you allow God to deepen these relationships. These are the people with whom you should gather.

The most important gathering of the church is the gathering of the Christian family. Jesus said there is unlimited power when only two will agree in prayer.[1] What power there can be when husband and wife come together in prayer! The most important gathering of the church is when you and your family gather together in your home for times of Bible study, sharing, worship, and prayer (more on this in Chapter 16).

We should be open to meet with any and all of God's people. There is only One Body. So let the Holy Spirit lead you day-by-day. Take nothing for granted. Do not lean on your own understanding.[2] He will lead you as to what group you are to gather with regularly and other groups which you should gather with from time-to-time. He will, also, cause your path to cross each day with those believers with whom you are to meet that day.

What Name to Gather In?

Most of Christendom gathers in some name—Baptist, Methodist, Pentecostal, etc. And, I'm afraid, too many of us in the house-church movement today gather as a *house-church*.

In Matthew 18:20, Jesus said, *"For where two or three have gathered together in My name, there I am in their midst."* The Greek Interlinear[3] has, *". . . having been assembled in my name. . ."* The Numeric English New Testament[4] reads, *". . . gathered unto My name. . ."*

We should come together in His Name, the Name of Jesus. We should gather unto Him, focus in on Him, center our hearts on Him, and allow Him to minister to us. He should be our focus. His Name should be what we have in common. We can come together in *one heart and one mind*[5] if we gather unto Him.

When to Gather?

When should we come together? In the early days of the Church they gathered daily.[6] By the time of the occurrence of Acts 20, there seemed to be a pattern of meeting on the *first day of the week*.[7] It would seem that by the time of the writing of the Revelation that this first day of the week had come to be known as the *Lord's day*.[8] Some considered a certain day more important than the other days, while others considered all days of equal importance.[9]

The important matter is not the specific day or time we come together. If He is the Lord of the Church (Chapter 2), and if we are His *ekklesia*, then we should look to Him to tell us when to gather. And we need to keep in mind that our spontaneous gatherings of *two or three*[10] on some downtown street corner may be just as significant as the meetings that are more regularly scheduled.

Why Gather?

Why is the church to *come together*, or *gather*, or *assemble*? Acts 13:2 tells of the church gathered together *"to minister to the Lord."* Hebrews 10:24-25 states that we are to come together *"to stimulate one another to love and good deeds"* and *"to encourage one another."* Here we have the two main purposes for which the church gathers: to minister to Him and to minister to one another. Nowhere do the Scriptures talk about gathering together to *have church*, or to *have a service*.

The following is a broader list of reasons why the church gathers and activities which might take place, as mentioned in the New Testament. (They are listed in the order they appear in the New Testament.)

- teaching – Acts 2:42; 1 Corinthians 14:26; 1 Timothy 4:13

- fellowship – Acts 2:42. The word *fellowship* is the English translation of the Greek word *koinonia*. It means *fellowship, association, community, communion, joint participation, intercourse, intimacy.*[11] Thus, fellowship is more than having a cup of coffee and some surface conversation together. It means to be in life together, walking deeply with one another.

- breaking bread (the Lord's Supper, communion) – Acts 2:42, 2:46, 20:7

- prayer – Acts 2:42, 12:12, 13:3

- sharing possessions with one another – Acts 2:44-45, 4:32-37

- having a meal together – Acts 2:46

- meeting the needs of the saints – Acts 6:1-6

- local leaders (elders and deacons) appointed – Acts 6:1-6, 14:23; 1 Timothy 3:1-13 (more on this in Chapter 12)

- ministry to the Lord – Acts 13:2

- fasting – Acts 13:2-3

- being spoken to by the Holy Spirit – Acts 13:2

- workers sent out – Acts 13:3 (more on this in Chapter 13)

- discussion – Acts 20:7 says Paul began *talking* to them. The Greek word is *dialegomai* and means *converse, discourse with one, argue, discuss, dialogue.*[12] Paul was not *preaching* to them; he was conversing with them.

- the Holy Spirit's gifts, or manifestations – 1 Corinthians 12-14

- edifying one another – 1 Corinthians 14:3-5, 12, 26; 1 Thessalonians 5:11

- singing – 1 Corinthians 14:26

- receiving a revelation – 1 Corinthians 14:26

- offerings taken for specific purposes – 1 Corinthians 16:1-3 (more on this in Chapter 17)

- encouraging one another – 1 Thessalonians 5:11; Hebrews 10:25

- reading the Scriptures – 1 Timothy 4:13

- exhortation – 1 Timothy 4:13

- stimulating one another to love and good deeds – Hebrews 10:24

Two Different Formats

There are two distinct kinds of gatherings in the New Testament. In Acts 2:41-42, we see the apostles teaching the three thousand new converts. Here we have a teacher-student format; a few teaching and many learning. This teacher-student format is for the instructing of the new convert, teaching them the basics of the Christian faith and life, which are mentioned in Hebrews 6:1-2. This should last for only a short period of time.

The format that God has in mind for His people after this brief, basic instruction is **not** a pulpit-pew, teacher-student format, **but a gathering** more in a circle-type of format, **where everyone can share in ministry and the group can function as a body.**

Paul's most extensive teaching on the Church is found in 1 Corinthians and Ephesians.[13] In 1 Corinthians he deals with the problem of division (chapters 1-4); the problem of immorality (chapter 5); the problem of lawsuits (chapter 6); the subject of marriage (chapter 7); and Christian freedom versus the conscience of others (chapters 8-10). In chapters 11-14, he teaches about the Church gathered. Chapter 15 deals with the subject of the resurrection, and chapter 16 closes with the letter.

In 11:1-16, he teaches about men, women, and head coverings; and in 11:17-34, the Lord's Supper. In chapter 12, he compares the Church to a human body, explaining that every part is **different**, is **important**, and is **to function**. In chapter 13, he says that all of this is to take place in an atmosphere of love. In chapter 14, verses 1-25, he deals with the proper exercise of the gifts of prophesy, tongues, and interpretation of tongues. In 14:26-40, we find Paul's concluding statements about the church gathered.

In 1 Corinthians 14:26 he says, *"What is the outcome then, brethren? When you assemble, each one has a psalm, has a teaching, has a revelation, has a tongue, has an interpretation. Let all things be done for edification."* Paul's other extensive teaching on the Church is the Book of Ephesians. In Ephesians 4:16, he states, *". . . from whom the whole body, being fitted and held together by that which every joint supplies, according to the proper working of each individual part, causes the growth of the body for the building up of itself in love"* (underscores added for emphasis). **If the Church is gathering according to God's plan, it will function as a**

body, with many of God's people ministering as the Holy Spirit gifts and leads them. Some may think that this does away with teaching. It doesn't. But the teaching flows along with all of the other ministries in the context of the church functioning as a body.

This everyone-involved type of gathering happens very naturally when believers gather in homes and sit in the normal seating of the home. Please don't drag in a pulpit and put the chairs in rows!

Sometimes the everyone-participating, normal gathering of the church is altered a bit if a traveling apostle, prophet, or teacher comes through your area and meets with you. Then the everyone-participate gathering allows room for the brother or sister to share, as took place in Acts 20:7-11. Room was made in the gathering for Paul to share. But he did not *take over* or monopolize. In fact, the Greek word, as we have already seen, means *converse, discourse, argue, discuss, dialogue.* He dialogued with them. He talked, but they also participated.

This author has been in many gatherings for over twenty-five years which functioned according to 1 Corinthians 14:26 and where the Holy Spirit was allowed to be in charge. There is nothing more beautiful or exciting! One never knows what the Lord has in mind. You come together, allow Him to lead, allow the many-membered body to function, and see what He develops. When the time is over, you can look back and see a theme that the Holy Spirit developed in your midst and you can say, "Oh, that's what God was saying to us today!"

What About *Preaching*?

This may be a surprise to some, but there is no place for *preaching* in the gathering of the saints. There are five Greek words that have all been translated into the English word *preach* and all similarly mean *herald, publish, announce, proclaim, tell* the Good News. All of the instances where these Greek words are found in the New Testament are in the context of announcing the Good News to the lost and are **not** found in the setting of the believers' gathering.

Preaching is to take place out where the lost are—door-to-door, the streets, the market place, the fields, the highways and by-ways. Some examples of preaching in the Scriptures are found in Matthew 3:1; Luke 9:6; Acts 5:42, 8:4, 25, 40; 11:20, and 20:25. We will deal further with *preaching* in Chapter 14.

So here is the *church gathered*—to minister to Him and to one another. The next chapter looks at the *church scattered*.

Chapter 6 Notes

1. Matthew 18:19
2. Proverbs 3:5-6
3. The *Greek-English New Testament* (based on *Nestle's Greek New Testament*), Christianity Today, Washington Building, Washington DC 20005, 1975, p. 61.
4. The *New Testament from the Greek Text as Established by Bible Numerics*, edited by Ivan Panin, The Book Society of Canada, Toronto, Canada, 1914. This is the life's work of Mr. Panin, based on the theory that every word in the original Bible has a numerical value which helps determine an accurate translation.
5. Acts 1:14, 2:46, 4:24, 32, 5:12, 15:25; Romans 12:16, 15:5; Philippians 1:27, 2:2
6. Acts 2:46, 5:42
7. Acts 20:7
8. Revelation 1:10
9. Romans 14:5-6; Colossians 2:16-23
10. Matthew 18:20
11. *Thayer's Greek-English Lexicon of the New Testament*, Baker Book House, Grand Rapids, Michigan, 1977, no. 2842.
12. *Thayer's*, no. 1256.
13. Galatians and Romans are teaching about salvation. 2 Corinthians is about how apostles should function. Philippians and Colossians are on practical Christian living. Philemon deals with the treatment of Onesimus. 1 Timothy and Titus have to do with appointing elders. 1 and 2 Thessalonians are about Christ's Return. 2 Timothy is Paul's farewell letter. Hebrews, which may or may not have been written by Paul, compares the Old and New Covenants.

7 | The Church Scattered

"Therefore, those who had been scattered went about preaching the word."   *—Acts 8:4*

The church *gathered* is the believers gathered together, worshiping Jesus, and encouraging one another. The church *scattered* is what believers do to influence and impact the world when they are not gathered. The *church scattered* is involved primarily in three activities: ministering mercy and compassion, evangelizing, and being a prophetic voice. This takes place all the time—in the neighborhood, the place of employment, and the market place.

Ministering His Love

Everywhere we go, believers are to minister love, mercy, compassion, and understanding; becoming all things to all men in order to reconcile them to Jesus.[1] This includes feeding the hungry, giving drink to the thirsty, inviting the stranger in, clothing the naked, visiting the sick and imprisoned, and visiting the orphans and widows.[2]

Sharing the Good News

We are also to be involved in sharing the Good News, witnessing and preaching wherever we go.[3] We see this in Jesus' life. He was touching lives everywhere He went, calling them to repent, and drawing them into His Kingdom. And we see it throughout the *Acts*—Peter, Philip, Paul, everyone, everywhere, every day sharing the Good News.[4] How important it is to be freshly empowered and led by God's Holy Spirit each day to be His effective witnesses.

Being a Prophetic Voice

As believers, we are also to be a prophetic voice to society; being salt (bringing seasoning) and light (bringing truth) everywhere we go.[5] We should be at the Holy Spirit's disposal to be a prophetic voice, a guiding light, a changing influence wherever we go—influencing the business transactions at our place of employment to be honest and fair; checking to see that the school board is promoting morality and a God-centered curriculum, not immorality and humanism; seeing that our neighbors are being treated fairly and kindly, regardless of race; working for a drug-free neighborhood; and encouraging a limited and just government.

We should also be standing up against abortion, homosexuality, pornography, divorce, child abuse, humanism, gambling, lotteries, greed, deception, immorality and all evil. Also, we should be attempting to release love, compassion, justice, righteousness, truth, mercy, joy, and peace everywhere we go.[6]

In some cases, our prophetic voice will best be heard by setting the example with our own separate institutions, i.e., home-schooling or

Christian schools, Christian businesses, and Christian communities.

At Your Place of Employment

An important place of ministry for each believer is his place of employment. It is one of the primary settings where we can minister God's love, share the Good News, and be a prophetic voice. And, let's not forget to do our work as if we were working for Jesus, and in a way that brings glory to the Father.[7]

In Conclusion

God only has one way to accomplish His purposes on this earth and that is through His people—those who will **go where He leads them and do what He tells them**. How important it is to be **led by His Spirit each day**; going where He leads, doing what He says, saying what He tells us to say! That's the church scattered!

Chapter 7 Notes

1. 1 Corinthians 9:19-23
2. Matthew 25:31-46; James 1:27
3. Some possible approaches to witnessing and evangelism include:
   a. Friendship evangelism
   b. Witnessing and soul winning opportunities throughout the day
   c. Distributing Gospel literature as part of your daily life
   d. Witnessing and distributing literature door-to-door
   e. Hospital visitation
   f. Retirement home visitation
   g. Telephone evangelism
   h. Contacting and following-up people referred by Christian television
   i. Open-air meetings
   j. Street witnessing
   k. Evangelism through drama and music
   l. Neighborhood Bible study groups
   m. Child Evangelism Clubs
   n. Tract racks in public places
   o. Prison work
   p. Military base work
4. Acts 5:42, 8:4, 25, 35; etc.
5. Matthew 5:13-16
6. A new magazine addressing the Church's role of being a prophetic voice to all of society is *Crosswinds*, P.O. Box A, Sunnyvale, California 94087
7. Colossians 3:23-24; Matthew 5:16

8 | Gathering in Homes

"The churches of Asia greet you. Aquila and Prisca greet you heartily in the Lord, with the church that is in their house."

−1 Corinthians 16:19

In the previous two chapters we have looked at the church—the *ekklesia*, the called-out ones, God's people—functioning in two settings, gathered and scattered. So where should the church gather? Tradition in most of the world would say that we should gather in *church* buildings. But what is God's plan? What do the Scriptures say?

What is the *House of God*?

Jesus said that true worship had nothing to do with a place and should flow from our hearts everywhere.[1] He also intimated that our bodies are the temple of God and are more important than buildings.[2] Jesus was (and is) the Son of God. He came to proclaim the Kingdom of God and to begin His Church. He was laying a new foundation for a new entity, the Church. It was very important that He set the right example and give the correct, foundational teaching. He never erected any buildings, nor did He instruct His followers to erect any buildings.

51

Stephen and Paul made it very clear that God does not dwell in buildings.[3] Paul said that we Christians are the temple.[4] Peter said that God is building a house of living stones (us!), not brick and mortar.[5]

What the Early Church Did

The first Christians in Jerusalem gathered in their homes.[6] They also gathered at Solomon's Temple, as was their habit as Jews, in order to proclaim Jesus as the Christ. But when they were thrown out of the Temple they made no attempt to build *church* buildings.

The following Scriptures show Christians everywhere gathering in their homes (underscore added for emphasis):

Acts 2:46 – *"And day by day continuing with one mind in the temple, and breaking bread from house to house, they were taking their meals together with gladness and sincerity of heart."*

Acts 5:42 – *"And every day, in the temple and from house to house, they kept right on teaching and preaching Jesus (as) the Christ."*

Acts 12:12 – *"And when he realized (this), he went to the house of Mary, the mother of John who was also called Mark, where many were gathered together and were praying."*

Acts 16:40 – *"And they went out of the prison and entered (the house of) Lydia, and when they saw the brethren, they encouraged them and departed."*

Acts 20:20 – ". . . *how I did not shrink from declaring to you anything that was profitable, and teaching you publicly and from <u>house to house</u>.*

Romans 16:3-5 – *"Greet Prisca and Aquila, my fellow workers in Christ Jesus, who for my life risked their own necks, to whom not only do I give thanks, but also all the churches of the Gentiles; also (greet) the <u>church that is in their house</u>. Greet Epaenetus, my beloved, who is the first convert to Christ from Asia."*

Romans 16:23 – *"Gaius, <u>host to me and to the whole church</u>, greets you. Erastus, the city treasurer greets you, and Quartus, the brother."*

1 Corinthians 16:19 – *"The churches of Asia greet you. Aquila and Prisca greet you heartily in the Lord, with the <u>church that is in their house</u>."*

Colossians 4:15 – *"Greet the brethren who are in Laodicea and also Nympha and the <u>church that is in her house</u>."*

Philemon 2 – ". . . *and to Apphia our sister, and to Archippus our fellow soldier, and to the <u>church in your house</u>."*

Do We Need Church Buildings?

It is this author's conviction that God never intended for believers to build *church* buildings. Judaism, in the Old Testament, was characterized by 1) sacrifices; 2) laws and regulations; 3) a special priesthood; and 4) buildings, i.e., the

Tabernacle in the wilderness, and later, the Temple in Jerusalem. **Jesus came to set God's people free from all four!** Under the New Covenant God's people no longer offer sacrifices, as Jesus has become our Sacrifice once for all. We are to be led by God's Spirit and His Word, rather than by laws and regulations. There is no special priesthood; we are all priests with direct access and accountability to God.[7] And, there is to be no special, set-apart place of worship called the *church*. **We are the *Church*.**

If God wanted us to be gathering in *church* buildings, would not Jesus have said something about this? Or Paul? Or Peter? Or somebody?? There is not one word in the entire New Testament about erecting special places of gathering called *churches*—not one! (It's interesting to note that whenever church buildings are dedicated today, appropriate Scripture is read from the Old Testament because there is none which can be read from the New Testament!) Believers are to come together in a very normal, natural place—their homes—to share their lives in Jesus with each other.

What God had in mind was **ordinary people**, gathering in **ordinary places** (their homes), to **share their lives with one another**. When the group gets too large for one home, simply divide and begin to meet in two homes. **What a simple, inexpensive, efficient way to multiply as we evangelize the world!** Sounds like God to me!

It is not clear how soon *church* buildings began to appear. Some sources indicate that there were very few until after Constantine became emperor in A.D. 312, and that it was his idea to erect

54

them.[8] Other sources indicate that there were buildings before A.D. 300.[9] The important point is that *church* buildings, whenever they appeared, were extra-biblical. There is not one word of Scripture that commands or gives any credence to them.

With the erecting of *churches*, **ordinary** people, gathering in **ordinary places**, to **share** their lives in Jesus with one another, became **special** people (the *clergy*), **conducting services** on Sunday morning in **special** places (the church building), and **Christianity was changed for 1700 years**.

Today, instead of sharing our lives with one another (experiencing *koinonia*), we have a religious production on a platform where a few perform and many observe. This has nothing to do with what Jesus was after. This is not the church that He came to build. It is a religious production. Jesus wants a functioning, interacting, many-membered Body, not an audience. **We need to repent of the work of man's hands and return to once again gathering in our homes in the humility, simplicity, and mutuality of the Early Church.**

What is Happening Today

Today God is leading His people back to the simple practice of gathering in their homes. Home groups have been popular for thirty years. House churches[10] have functioned for many years in cities like Singapore and Hong Kong where there is no room for *church* buildings. Today Christians are leaving the institutional church by the thousands all over the world and returning to the simple practice of gathering in their homes as the early Church did for several hundred years. It is a sovereign move of God! **God is getting His Church prepared for a coming, great, world-wide revival; a great ingathering of the harvest; and coming, end-time persecution.**

Some groups stay in the same home every week for continuity; some groups stay in the same home for a month, then move to another home; some groups move around to a different home each week. The Holy Spirit will show you what to do and how to do it.

A number of home church groups can always come together periodically for a larger, joint gathering. Coming together about every three months is a common pattern with some house church networks. You can gather on someone's property, in a park, or rent a hall for the day. Again, the Holy Spirit will lead you as to where and how often to come together.

What a simple way to evangelize the world, disciple new converts, experience *koinonia*, impact your neighborhood, influence society, and be the church in all respects—just gather in your home with other believers from your area. When the group grows too large for one home, divide, and meet in two. Keep growing, dividing, and multiplying until the entire world is evangelized!

Chapter 8 Notes

1. John 4:20-24
2. John 2:19-22
3. Acts 7:48, 17:24-25
4. 1 Corinthians 3:16-17, 6:19; 2 Corinthians 6:16; Ephesians 2:21-22
5. 1 Peter 2:5
6. Acts 2:46
7. 1 Peter 2:5, 9
8. One source we have on this is *Archaeological Evidence of Church Life Before Constantine*, by Graydon F. Snyder, the SeedSowers, P.O. Box 3368, Auburn, Maine 04212, 1985. On p. 67 he states that there is no literary or archaeological evidence of a church building prior to Constantine. Pages 68-71 tell of a home in the city of Dura-Europus, in today's Syria, that was remodeled between A.D. 232 and 256 to accommodate the church. A baptistry was added, and walls were moved to accommodate 65-75 persons. You are encouraged to consult this helpful volume. Another source is *The Open Church*, by James H. Rutz, Open Church Ministries, 333 Reddick Road, Portal, GA 30450, (333)OPEN 1-2-3, pp. 46-48.
9. Eusebius, in his writings, translated into *The History of the Church from Christ to Constantine*, by G.A. Williamson, Dorset Press, New York, NY, 1965, refers to church buildings prior to A.D. 300 on pp. 300, 319, 326, 330, 353-56, 373, 376-77, and 382-84. *A History of the Christian Church*, by Lars P. Qualben, Thomas Nelson, New York, NY, 1968, likewise, tells of buildings before A.D. 300. He states, "The earliest known church buildings were erected in Edessa, Arbela, and vicinity

before the year 200," p. 113. *A History of Christianity – Volume 1*, by Kenneth Latourette, Harper & Row, New York, NY, 1975, states, "a building which was used as a church at least as far back as the year 232," p. 79.

10. The terms *house church, house churches, home church*, and *church in the home* are used throughout this book to refer to any group of believers who gather on a regular basis in one or more homes and sees these home meetings as their primary place of fellowship in the Body of Christ.

9 | Everyone a Minister

"But to each one is given the manifestation of the spirit for the common good." –1 Corinthians 12:7

By tradition we are accustomed to *going to church* to hear the *minister*. But this is not what the Scriptures teach. The early Christians gathered in their homes (see Chapter 8). They had a group of leaders called *elders* (see Chapter 12). But they did not have a *minister*. In fact, they **all were ministers!**

Being Servants

There are six Greek words which have been translated into our English word *minister*. They all have the same basic meaning of *servant* or *to serve*. A few examples of how they are used in Scripture include:

Luke 3:23 – Jesus was about thirty when He began His *ministry*, i.e. His **giving of Himself** fully to the proclaiming of the Good News.

Matthew 4:11; Mark 1:13 – angels **served** Jesus at the end of His forty days of testing in the wilderness.

Matthew 27:55; Mark 15:41 – there were women who traveled with Jesus and the Twelve to **serve** them.

Acts 1:17, 1:25 – Judas once shared in the **place of service** that Jesus had allotted to the Twelve.

Acts 6:4 – the apostles felt the need to give themselves full-time to the **giving out** of the Word.

Acts 20:24 – Paul felt a certain **area of servanthood** which he had received from the Lord.

Acts 21:19 – Paul shared what God did among the Gentiles through his being faithful to the **area of servanthood** God had given him.

Acts 24:23 – Paul's friends **served** him while he was imprisoned.

Romans 11:13 – Paul made full use of his **service** to the Gentiles.

Romans 13:4 – governing authorities are **servants** of God.

1 Corinthians 12:5 – there are many different ways in which the Holy Spirit may equip one to **serve** the Body of Christ.

1 Corinthians 16:15 – the household of Stephanas **served** the saints.

2 Corinthians 3:1-11, 4:1, 6:3-10 – Paul writes about the apostolic **ministry** which he and others had.

2 Corinthians 5:17-21 – all believers are **given a ministry** of bringing others to Christ.

2 Corinthians 9:1, 12-13 – Paul exhorts the Corinthian believers to **serve** others by the giving of their finances.

Hebrews 1:14 – angels are to **serve** Christians.

Hebrews 10:11 – the Old Testament priests **gave** sacrifices to God.

We can see from these passages that the basic meaning of these Greek words is *to serve*, or *to be a servant.* All Christians are to be God's servants. Under the New Covenant, all believers are priests.[1] There are some Christians whom God may call to give themselves full-time *to prayer and to the ministry of the Word.*[2] And there are those whom the risen Christ has gifted as an apostle, prophet, evangelist, shepherd, or teacher.[3] But nowhere do the Scriptures talk about *the minister* that one is to go hear every Sunday.

Minister to God

All believers are to *minister* in three directions: to God, to one another, and to the world. We all are to minister to God. Acts 13:2 says,

> And while they were ministering to the Lord and fasting, the Holy Spirit said, "Set apart for Me Barnabas and Saul for the work to which I have called them."

We are to love Him, worship Him, praise Him, thank Him, serve Him, obey Him, wait upon Him, look to Him, trust Him, petition Him, etc.

Minister to One Another

We all are to minister to one another. We are to:

- be at peace with one another – Mark 9:50

- converse with one another – Luke 24:17, 32

- love (lay our lives down for) one another – John 13:34-35, 15:12, 15:17

- share our possessions with one another – Acts 4:32-35

- recognize that we are actually members of one another – Romans 12:5; Ephesians 4:25

- be devoted to one another – Romans 12:10

- give preference and honor to one another – Romans 12:10

- be of the same mind toward (live in harmony with) one another – Romans 12:16, 15:5

- do not owe one another – Romans 13:8

- not judge one another – Romans 14:13, 19

- accept one another – Romans 15:7

- admonish one another – Romans 15:14

- greet one another with a holy kiss – Romans 16:16; 1 Corinthians 16:20; 2 Corinthians 13:12; 1 Peter 5:14

- do not sue one another – 1 Corinthians 6:7

- when you come together to eat, wait for one another – 1 Corinthians 11:33

- care for one another – 1 Corinthians 12:25

- serve one another – Galatians 5:13

- do not devour one another – Galatians 5:15

- do not challenge one another or envy one another – Galatians 5:26

- bear one another's burdens – Galatians 6:2

- with all humility and gentleness, with patience, show forbearance to one another in love – Ephesians 4:2

- be kind to one another, tender-hearted, forgiving each other – Ephesians 4:32

- speak to one another in psalms, hymns, and spiritual songs – Ephesians 5:19; Colossians 3:16

- submit (defer, yield) to one another – Ephesians 5:21

- regard one another with importance – Philippians 2:3-4

- do not lie to one another – Colossians 3:9

- bear with one another, forgive each other – Colossians 3:13

- abound in love for one another – 1 Thessalonians 4:9

- comfort one another – 1 Thessalonians 4:18

- encourage one another, build up one another – 1 Thessalonians 5:11

- live in peace with one another – 1 Thessalonians 5:13

- do not repay evil for evil to one another but always seek that which is good for one another – 1 Thessalonians 5:15

- encourage one another – Hebrews 3:13, 10:25

- stimulate one another to love and good deeds – Hebrews 10:24

- do not speak against one another – James 4:11

- do not complain against one another – James 5:9

- confess our sins to one another and pray for one another – James 5:16

- love one another fervently from the heart – 1 Peter 1:22

- be hospitable to one another – 1 Peter 4:9

- use your spiritual gifts to serve one another – 1 Peter 4:10

- have humility toward one another – 1 Peter 5:5

- be in fellowship with one another – 1 John 1:7

- love one another – 1 John 3:11, 3:23, 4:7, 4:11, 4:12, 2 John 1:5

When the Church Gathers, Every Believer is to Minister

Every believer should look to the Lord as to how He might want to use him or her to bring edification and blessing to the Body. 1 Corinthians 14:26 states,

> When you assemble, each one has a psalm, has a teaching, has a revelation, has a tongue, has an interpretation. Let all things be done for edification.

And Ephesians 4:16 talks about the Body *"Building itself up in love"* by *"that which every joint supplies"* and by *"the proper working of each individual part."*

Minister to the World

And we are to minister to the world: we are to minister Christ's love, mercy and compassion; we are to evangelize; and we are to be a prophetic voice (see Chapter 7).

In Conclusion

There is not a special class of Christians called *ministers.* There are some believers to whom God has given a special anointing and area of responsibility and servanthood as an apostle, prophet, evangelist, shepherd, or teacher.[4] (More on this in Chapter 13.) And there are those whom God leads to be involved in that servanthood on a full-time basis.[5] But this does not mean a special class or category called *clergy* or *minister.* All believers are ministers, servants—to God, to fellow believers, and to the world.

Chapter 9 Notes

1. 1 Peter 2:5, 9
2. Acts 6:4
3. Ephesians 4:11
4. Ephesians 4:8-11
5. Acts 6:4

10 | The Holy Spirit's Role

"And behold, I am sending forth the promise of My Father upon you; but you are to stay in the city until you are clothed with power from on high."   *–Luke 24:49*

There is one indispensable ingredient to living a successful Christian life and to seeing the Church function as God intended: **the full and free moving of the Holy Spirit.**

In Chapter 4 we dealt with the two great experiences of being *born of the Spirit* and being *baptized in the Holy Spirit.* Being born of the Spirit and baptized in the Spirit should be followed by additional *fillings,* when the Holy Spirit freshly fills the believer with a new empowering for each new situation.[1] Continuing to walk in His fullness necessitates our obeying the Spirit; and not grieving or quenching His presence in our lives.[2] Hopefully, one would learn to receive fresh infillings in such a way, that he would always be *full of the Holy Spirit.*[3]

There are seven purposes for, or results of, the filling ministry of the Holy Spirit.

1. To Cleanse the Inner Man In Acts 15:8-9, the Scriptures talk about the cleansing of the heart by the Holy Spirit. It is this great truth of cleansing, or sanctification, that the Holiness movement has historically taught. The Holy Spirit will cleanse your inner man as you surrender to His infilling.

2. To Give Power to Live the Victorious Christian Life Romans 8; Galatians 5:16, 25; and other Scriptures, tell of the life of victory that is available to the believer who is filled with the Spirit. This has been the message of the Keswick movement for over one hundred years. We can walk in victory each day as we walk yielded to the Spirit's control and leading.

3. To Give Power to Witness The Holy Spirit is the *Lord of the Harvest*.[4] Luke 24:47-49, Acts 1:8, and Acts 4:31, tell us of the boldness and fruitfulness in evangelism which comes to the believer who has been baptized with the Holy Spirit. It's as we are daily empowered and led by Him that we will see Him touch lives and society through us.

4. The Fruit of the Spirit Galatians 5:22-23 tells of that gracious fruit which characterizes the life of the Spirit-filled believer. It includes:

love	patience	faithfulness
joy	kindness	gentleness
peace	goodness	self-control

This fruit does not occur in our lives by our striving to attain it, but rather, by our releasing our lives to His control; then He will naturally produce it.

5. The Gifts of the Spirit There are a number of ways which the Holy Spirit may gift or equip us to serve and bless those around us. They are listed in the Bible in four lists and several other individual passages. We include them here, with a brief explanation of each, as follows:

Romans 12:6-8
- Prophecy – proclaiming God's truth
- Service – meeting practical needs
- Teaching – clarifying truth
- Exhorting – stimulating faith
- Giving – distributing material resources
- Leading – coordinating the activities of others
- Showing mercy – bearing another's burden

1 Corinthians 12:8-10
- Word of wisdom – a wise word of counsel, inspired by God
- Word of knowledge – God-revealed information
- Faith – assurance of what God wants to do
- Healings – the power of God restoring health
- Effecting miracles – God intervening in the course of nature
- Prophecy – a supernatural utterance in a known language
- Distinguishing of spirits – discerning whether spirit activity is from God, self, or Satan
- Tongues – a supernatural utterance in a language not known by the speaker
- Interpretation of tongues – the supernatural revealing of the meaning of an utterance in tongues

Ephesians 4:11
- Apostle – one sent forth

- Prophet – a proclaimer of God's truth, primarily to believers
- Evangelist – a proclaimer of God's truth, primarily to non-believers
- Shepherd – one who cares for God's people
- Teacher – one who unfolds God's truth, primarily to believers

1 Corinthians 12:28
- Helps – assists those in leadership
- Administrations – one who guides/pilots projects

1 Corinthians 13:3
- Martyrdom – the gift of suffering and dying

1 Corinthians 7:7
- Celibacy – the gift of being single

We are indebted to the Pentecostal/ Charismatic movement for the proclamation of this aspect of the Spirit's work. As we surrender to the Holy Spirit, experience His fullness, and obey His promptings, He will equip, or gift, each of us in the ways He wants us to bless His Body and the world.[5]

6. To be Led by the Spirit Acts 8:29, 16:6-7, and Romans 8:14 tell of the believer being directed, or led, by the Spirit. How important it is to learn to discern His voice. Then we can be told by Him each day where to go, what to do, and what to say.

7. To Equip the Body to Function Our Lord's Church is not to operate using the talent and strength of the natural man. **The Church functions as God designed when the Holy Spirit is allowed to freely and completely fill, anoint, gift, and move in and through all of the**

believers who are assembled together. When He is allowed to fill each believer, and when He is allowed to be in active control of the believers' gatherings, then He will flow in mighty cleansing, empowering, and leading, distributing an abundance of His fruit, gifts, and ministries. We must allow the Holy Spirit, not man, to lead and anoint our times together. It is a group of believers who have experienced His baptism of power, and are being led by Him, who will experience His highest and best.

All seven of these purposes are to **glorify Jesus.**[6]

In Conclusion

Paramount to everything is His **fullness** and **leading**. It is His fullness which releases God's highest and best to each of us. If we do anything without His fullness and leading, we are walking and serving God in the flesh. It is so easy to go forth and do much activity in the flesh, and it's simply *"wood, hay, and straw."*[7] Jesus told His first followers *"to stay in the city until you are clothed with power from on high."*[8] In other words, don't go forth to do anything until you have His fullness. God's purposes can only come to pass through those of His followers who are walking in His fullness and are being intimately, constantly led by Him. If we want to do God's word God's way, we're going to have to learn to wait upon Him; experience and walk in His fullness; and be clearly led, step-by-step, by His Spirit. Then we will see His will done in and through His Church—gathered and scattered.

Chapter 10 Notes

1. Acts 4:8, 31; Ephesians 5:18
2. Acts 5:32; Ephesians 4:30; 1 Thessalonians 5:19
3. Acts 6:3, 5
4. Matthew 9:38
5. 1 Corinthians 12:4-7; 1 Peter 4:10; Acts 5:32
6. John 15:26, 16:14
7. 1 Corinthians 3:12
8. Luke 24:49

11 | Women –
Equal Partners

"Even upon My bondslaves, both men and women, I will in those days pour forth of My Spirit, and they shall prophesy."   *–Acts 2:18*

One cannot write a book on the subject of God's plan for His Church without looking at His plan for women. After all, they are about fifty percent of the human race—and should comprise about half of the Church! The subject of God's plan for women is much debated today; both with regard to the subject of authority in the marriage relationship and with regard to the ministry of women in the Church.

On one side we have those who teach that man is to have authority over his wife. This view is usually based on the fact that the man was created first, and on the understanding that the Greek word *kephale*, translated *head* in 1 Corinthians 11:3 and Ephesians 5:23, means *authority over*. People of this persuasion usually hold to a restricted role for women in the Church based on their understanding of 1 Corinthians 14:34-36 and 1 Timothy 2:11-15.[1]

On the other side are those who teach that husband and wife are to walk as equals, submitted to one another, and to the Lord, based on Ephesians 5:21, and on their understanding that the Greek word *kephale* means *source of life* rather than *authority over.*[2] Those of this persuasion usually have a more releasing understanding of God's place for women in His Church.[3]

This writer has the latter understanding and will try to briefly explain it in this chapter. We will deal first with the husband-wife relationship and then with the place of women in the Church.

In the Home

It was God's intention that man and woman be equal from the very beginning: they were both to *rule.*[4] Then God took one side (not *rib* as most translations have it) of Adam to form Eve.[5] She was made to be *"a helper suitable for* (or *corresponding to*) *him."*[6] Eve was not made to be Adam's *helper* in the sense of a servant, but in the sense of a spiritual help and an assisting partner.[7] The phrase *corresponding to* is the Hebrew word *neged*, and means *in front of, in sight of, in the presence of, before, over against, opposite.*[8] Eve was made to be a corresponding part for Adam; standing before him, being in his presence, being his opposite; they matched each other, like two pieces of a jig-saw puzzle.

After the Fall, God's ultimate plan of partnership did not change. However, because of the Fall, Adam would have a tendency to rule his wife. God warned Eve, *"He will rule over you."*[9]

In Proverbs 31, we see *"the excellent wife"* as one who not only cared for the needs of her family, but was involved in finding a field and buying it, planting a vineyard, and extending her hand to the poor and needy—all of which involved the exercise of authority.

The Ephesians 5:21-33 passage, so crucial to this subject, begins with verse 15: walk wisely, use your time carefully, understand God's will, be filled with the Spirit, etc., and, verse 21, *"be subject to one another in the fear of Christ."* This word *subject* or *submit* is from the Greek word *hupotasso,* and means *to place, arrange, or rank under; to subject, to subordinate, to obey; to submit to one's control; to yield to one's admonition or advice.*[10] Although the word includes a dimension of obedience it is more a heart attitude of yieldedness than a blind obedience. One author has this interesting comment:

> Two words are constantly confused in reference to woman's duties, *subjection* and *obedience* . . . The noun *subjection* is not found (in Classical Greek) outside the New Testament, and we are left to infer that it was coined to describe a relation peculiar to believers. Had the word merely meant *obedience,* such an invention would have been needless . . . The true sense of the word describes the Christian grace of yielding one's preferences to another, where principle is not involved, rather than asserting one's rights.[11]

The husband and wife, in *"being subject to one another"* (verse 21) are to *place themselves under the control of* the other; they are to yield to the desires and advice of the other.[12]

The Greek word *kephale,* translated *head* in verse 23, has traditionally been interpreted *authority over.* But there is another Greek word

75

most commonly used for authority, *exousia*. Recent scholarship indicates that *kephale* more probably means *source of life*. If this is true, then the husband is to be an encouraging, empowering *source of life* to his wife, just as Christ is the source of life and power for His Church. The same meaning would hold true for *head* in 1 Corinthians 11:3. (The debate over the meaning of *kephale* or *head* is far from over!) This much we can clearly say: the husband is to lay his life down for his wife,[13] and the wife is to submit to and respect her husband.[14]

With regard to the wife's authority and responsibility to manage the home, 1 Timothy 5:14 says that widows are to *"get married, bear children, keep house. . ."* The Greek word for *keep house* (a very poor rendering of the Greek) is *oikodespoteo*, and means to *rule a household* or *be the master of a house*.[15] God intends for a wife to *rule, master, run, manage the home*. In too many homes the wife manages the home until the husband walks in, then he takes over. This should not be. Dear husbands, release your wife to manage the home!

In the Church

With regard to the matter of God's design for women in His Church, I would begin by saying that it is fairly obvious that the majority of leadership in both the Old and the New Testaments was male. However, there is enough evidence of God using women in both ministry and leadership in both Testaments, as we will see, that man should not in any way restrict what

God might choose to do today through any woman.

Let's take a look at some of the ways which God used women in the Old Testament. Moses' and Aaron's sister Miriam was a prophetess and one of the leaders of the children of Israel along with her two brothers.[16] The inheritance laws were changed after the daughters of Zelophehad appealed to Moses and he sought God about the matter.[17] Deborah, a prophetess, who was *"judging Israel at this time"*; had *"the word of the Lord"* for the army general Barak; and went to battle with him at his request.[18]

God used Abigail to provide for David and his men, contrary to her husband's wishes, but with God's blessing.[19] During Judah's closing days, the King's priest was sent to Huldah to get *"the word of the Lord"* for the King and the people even though Jeremiah and Zephaniah were both available at that time.[20]

With the inauguration of the Church Age, God has something even more clear in mind: the full liberation of all people into a *one new man* which eliminates all previous distinctions of race, nationality, social, and economic status, and sex.[21]

In Acts 2:17-18, Peter, quoting from Joel 2, says,

> "And it shall be in the last days," God says, "That I will pour forth of My Spirit upon all flesh; And your <u>sons and your daughters</u> shall prophesy, And your young men shall see visions, And your old men shall dream dreams; Even upon My bondslaves, <u>both men and women</u>, I will in those days pour forth of My

Spirit. And they shall prophesy." (Underscore
added for emphasis.)

It is God's intention that male and female
were to have an equal role during the Church
Age and that He was pouring His Spirit forth on
both, to equally fill both, to equally equip both
for their place of ministry.

The gifts of the Spirit are for both, and they
are both to function as members of the body,
without any distinction made between male and
female.[22] 1 Corinthians 14:26 and Ephesians 4:16
make no distinction between men and women in
their ministry of having a psalm, teaching,
revelation, speaking in tongues and interpreting,
and being part of the body that builds itself up in
love by that which every joint (the joining
together of two parts, making no distinction
between male and female) supplies, by the
proper working of each individual part (male
and female).

1 Corinthians 14:34-38 is not a very clear
passage, and many explanations have been given
as to its meaning.[23] One cannot build the whole
doctrine of the place of women in the Church
from this passage, which is not very clear.

1 Timothy 2:11-15 is the other passage usually
strongly emphasized in attempting to restrict the
place of women in the Church. It, likewise, is not
an easy passage to understand; and a number of
explanations have been given. It is this writer's
understanding that this is dealing with a local
situation and encourages the women to be
instructed in the ways of God as new converts
before they attempt to teach others. The Greek

word, usually translated *exercise authority over* in verse 12, is *authentein*. It only appears this one time in the entire New Testament. Recent scholarship indicates that the meaning of this Greek word in Paul's day had nothing to do with authority, but meant either *to commit murder*, or denoted *loose sexual behavior practiced in pagan worship*.[24] So again, we can't build doctrine primarily on this passage of Scripture which is, likewise, not clear.

With regard to the gifting of women by the risen Christ for special ministries (Ephesians 4:8-11), we see Junia, a woman **apostle**, mentioned in Romans 16:7.[25] It is also significant how many times throughout Church history God used women to plant churches and found various other Christian institutions, i.e., orphanages, monasteries, mission agencies, and denominations.[26] Philip had four daughters who were **prophet**esses.[27] Psalms 68:11 probably speaks of female **evangelists**. Jesus first appeared to women after His resurrection and gave them the task of first proclaiming that He had risen.[28] 2 John 1, *"the chosen lady,"* is probably referring to a female **shepherd**. And in Acts 18:26 we see Priscilla functioning as a **teacher**.

Priscilla and Aquila are an interesting couple. Of the six times in Scripture[29] that their names are mentioned together, four of the times Priscilla's name is mentioned first, which indicates that, in those four instances, she was the leader of their husband-wife ministry team.[30]

For further evidence of God using women during New Testament times, we see Paul calling Priscilla and Aquila his *"fellow workers in Christ*

Jesus."[31] He similarly refers to Euodia and Syntyche as *"fellow workers."*[32] 1 Corinthians 1:11 speaks of *Chloe's people*, probably a church that met in her home.[33] Many of the home churches in the first three centuries met in the homes of women. Whatever home the gathering was in, that person was usually part of the leadership of the group.[34] The possibility of women elders and deacons is dealt with in Chapter 12.

In Conclusion

This writer's understanding of Scripture is that God did away with all of the distinctions in His Church which had separated people for centuries: circumcision, national, racial, social, economic, and sexual. In so doing, He released all to be part of a new entity, *one new man*: so that all could freely function under the Holy Spirit's anointing and leadership.[35]

In 1 Peter 3:7, Peter says, *". . . grant her honor as a fellow heir of the grace of life. . ."* Various translations render *fellow heir* as *joint heirs, heirs, you share together, partners, fellow inheritors, together with you, heirs together, heirs with you, she shares with you.* This certainly sounds to me like partners in life together! So we have men and women as complimentary, equal partners in God's plan for His Church: equal partners in the home, equal partners in the functioning of the church, equal partners in ministry, and equal partners in church leadership.

In closing this chapter, I appeal to you, dear husband, quit ruling your wife. Let Jesus be her Lord, not you. Treat her as your equal. Lay your life down for her and release her to be all that God wants her to be. And, I appeal to you, dear spiritual leaders, don't *handcuff* half of God's army. Release the women to be all that God wants them to be in His Church.

Chapter 11 Notes

1. A very comprehensive presentation of this position is given in the recently published book, *Recovering Biblical Manhood and Womanhood*, edited by John Piper and Wayne Grudem, Crossway Books, Wheaton, Illinois 60187, 1991, 566 pp.

2. See note 3 in Chapter 2.

3. The equality in marriage and broader role for women in the Church position can be researched further by studying the following: *A Response to the Danvers Statement*, by R.K. McGregor Wright, Christians for Biblical Equality, St. Paul, Minnesota 55107, 1989; *Beyond Sex Roles*, by Gilbert Bilezikian, Baker Book House, Grand Rapids, Michigan 49516, 1985; *Call Me Blessed*, by Faith Martin, Eerdmans Publishing, Grand Rapids, Michigan 49503, 1988; *Church Leadership*, by Lawrence Richards & Clyde Hoeldtke, Zondervan, Grand Rapids, Michigan 49506, 1980, pp. 16-26; *Does* Kephale *Mean* Source *or* Authority Over *in Greek Literature?*, by Richard S. Cervin, available from Christians for Biblical Equality; *God's Word to Women*, by Katharine C. Bushnell, published by Ray Munson, Box 417, North Collins, New York 14111 (originally published in 1921); *I Suffer Not a Woman: Rethinking 1 Timothy 2:11-15*, by Richard and Catherine Kroeger, Baker Book House, Grand Rapids, Michigan 49516, 1992; *In Search of God's Ideal Woman*, by Dorothy R. Pape, InterVarsity Press, Downers Grove, Illinois 60515, 1979; *WOMAN–God's Plan, not Man's Tradition*, by Joanne Krupp, 2121 Barnes Ave. SE, Salem, Oregon 97306; *Men, Women & Biblical Equality*,

Christians for Biblical Equality; *Paul, Women & Wives*, by Crain S. Keener, Hendrickson Publishers, Peabody, Massachusetts 01961-3473, 1992; *The House Church*, by Del Birkey, Herald Press, Scottdale, Pennsylvania 15683, 1988, pp. 91-103; *Who Said Women Can't Teach?*, by Charles Trombley, Bridge Publishing, South Plainfield, New Jersey 07080, 1985; and *Women, Authority & the Bible*, edited by Alvera Mickelsen, InterVarsity Press, Downers Grove, Illinois 60515, 1986. These and other resources are available from Christians for Biblical Equality, 380 Lafayette Road S, Suite 122, St. Paul, Minnesota 55107-1216.

4. Genesis 1:26

5. Genesis 1:27, 2:18-25, 5:1-2. *Rib* is the Hebrew word *tsela* and is found 52 times in the Old Testament. It is translated *rib* only twice, in Genesis 2:21-22. Most frequently it is translated *side* (26 times), and *chambers* (11 times)—from *NASB Concordance* and *Gesenius' Lexicon*, no. 6763.

6. Genesis 2:18

7. Most frequently the words *help* and *helper* refer to God as our helper, or to one group of people assisting or aiding another—*Gesenius'*, no 5826, 5828, and 5833.

8. *Gesenius'*, no. 5048.

9. Genesis 3:16. Most translations render it *"He shall rule over you,"* as if it is a command from God to Adam that he is to rule his wife. A more accurate rendering is *will*, indicating to Eve that fallen Adam would have a tendency to rule her. For a thorough treatment of this subject in Genesis, chapters 2-3, see *WOMAN–God's Plan, not Man's Tradition*, by Joanne Krupp, 2121 Barnes Ave. SE, Salem, Oregon 97306.

10. *NASB Concordance* and *Thayer's Lexicon*, no. 5293.

11. *God's Word to Women*, Katherine C. Bushnell, published by Ray B. Munson, P.O. Box 417, North Collins, New York 14111, p. 292.

12. *Thayer's*, no. 5293.

13. Ephesians 5:25-29, 33

14. Ephesians 5:22-24, 33

15. *Thayer's*, no. 3616.

16. Micah 6:4

17. Numbers 27:1-11

18. Judges 4:4-23

19. 1 Samuel 25

20. 2 Kings 22:8-20; Jeremiah 1:1-2; Zephaniah 1:1

21. Acts 2:16-18; Ephesians 2:11-22; Galatians 3:23-29

22. 1 Corinthians 12-14

23. One possible explanation that this writer feels comfortable with is the following: *"Just as the Law also says"* (verse 34) does not seem to be referring to any Old Testament passage. It may be referring to the Jewish oral law. This, and verse 35, may be a quote to Paul in the letter he was answering. If this is true, then Paul is saying that women, contrary to the teaching of the Jewish oral law, are to minister. Verse 36 – the Word of God can go forth from women as well as men. Verse 37-38 – Paul's teachings of liberation and release for all need to be received. Verses 39-30 – all may prophesy and speak in tongues, if done in an orderly manner. There are other plausible explanations for 1 Corinthians 14:34-38, which are given in the various books which are recommended in footnotes one and three.

24. *Who Said Women Can't Teach?*, Charles Trombley, Bridge Publishing, South Plainfield, New Jersey, 1985, pp. 176-78.

25. Present day translations and authorities are about equally divided on whether this is a female name *Junia*, or a male name *Junias*. However, a number of the Church fathers understood it to be feminine, including Origen (A.D. 185-253), Chrysostom (347-407), and Jerome (304-419). Dr. Leonard Swidler, in his *Biblical Affirmations of Women*, Westminster Press, Philadelphia, Pennsylvania, 1979, p. 299, says, "To the best of my knowledge, no commentator on the text until Aegidus of Rome (A.D. 1245-1316) took the name to be masculine."

26. This is well documented in Ruth Tucker's book *Daughters of the Church*, Zondervan Publishing, Grand Rapids, Michigan 49506, 1987.

27. Acts 21:9

28. Matthew 28:1-10; Mark 16:1-11; John 20:1-18

29. Acts 18:2, 18, 26; Romans 16:3; 1 Corinthians 16:19; and 2 Timothy 4:19

30. The order of names in Scripture is significant. An example is Paul and Barnabas. Their names are listed *Barnabus and Saul* in Acts 13:1-7 but *Paul and Barnabas* starting in 13:42. God switched the leadership role, or function, between them.

31. Romans 16:3

32. Philippians 4:3

33. 1 Corinthians 1:11

34. Trombley, p. 189.

35. Ephesians 2:11-22; Galatians 3:23-29; Acts 2:16-18; 1 Corinthians 12-14.

12 | Leadership –
Elders and Deacons

". . . to all the saints in Christ Jesus who are in Philippi, including the overseers (elders) and deacons." —*Philippians 1:1*

Jesus' Words About Leaders

Much is said today about leaders. One often hears statements like, "Who's in charge here?," "Who is your leader?," or "Whose church is this?" It's interesting what Jesus said about *leaders*:

> And they love the place of honor at banquets, and the chief seats in the synagogues, and respectful greetings in the market places, and being called by men, Rabbi. But do not be called Rabbi; for <u>One is your Teacher</u>, and <u>you are all brothers</u>. And do not call anyone on earth your father; for One is your Father, He who is in heaven. And <u>do not be called leaders; for One is your Leader</u>, that is, Christ (Matthew 23:6-10, underscore added for emphasis).

It sounds different from our present-day practice of calling people *father, reverend, minister, pastor, director, executive director,* and *president*. We all want our titles and positions of authority rather than humbling ourselves and just being brothers.

Jesus also had something to say about hierarchies of authority:

> You know that the rulers of the Gentiles lord it over them, and their great men exercise authority over them. It is not so among you, but whoever wishes to become great among you shall be your servant, and whoever wishes to be first among you shall be your slave; just as the Son of Man did not come to be served, but to serve, and to give His life a ransom for many (Matthew 20:25-28, underscore added for emphasis).

In the world (corporate world, military, etc.) there are chains-of-command, organizational charts, and hierarchies of authority. But Jesus said it's not to be that way in His Kingdom. **In His Kingdom we are to be brothers (and sisters), laying our lives down for one another, and being led by One Leader, Jesus.**

Why Leadership?

There is a reason for true spiritual leadership: to lay our life down for others, being a servant of all, **encouraging God's people to each be led clearly by Him alone.** In any situation, leadership is there to be watchmen, to try to ensure: (1) that the **Lordship of Jesus Christ is not hindered**, (2) that the **free moving of the Holy Spirit is not hampered,** and (3) that **every believer is released to be a free, active, functioning, member of the Body.** Much of the time, true spiritual leaders, having released the people of God to minister, serve as *invisible*

leaders, staying out of the way so that the Body can function.

Spiritual leadership should be sought from those who are the most mature. In the world, the person who talks the most, is the most forceful, and is able to manipulate others, often does the leading. This should not be the case in Christ's Church. The leaders in His Church should be those mature, broken, humble, deeply spiritual veterans who have walked with the Holy Spirit for years. They will not promote themselves into leadership. Their wisdom and mature leadership should be sought after.

So what about all of the titles we see in the New Testament—apostle, prophet, evangelist, pastor/shepherd, teacher, elder, deacon? And what about *ordination*?

Apostle, prophet, evangelist, shepherd, and teacher are not offices, positions, or titles. They are functions; they are giftings. The risen Christ may anoint someone to be a shepherd and give him as His gift to the Body of Christ. That person is a shepherd, functioning in the body. He is not in a separate class, called clergy; nor should he be called *Reverend* (only One is reverend!), nor does he now have a title *Pastor*. If Jesus anoints someone to be an evangelist, likewise, that one is just an ordinary person, part of the body, who is always very naturally leading people to Jesus and equipping the body to reach others. Not special people, put in a special class, with a special title; but ordinary people, gifted by the risen Christ and given to the Church to serve God's people, equipping them all for ministry.

(More on the apostle, prophet, evangelist, shepherd, and teacher in Chapter 13.)

Elders

There are two, and only two, offices that we find mentioned in the New Testament—elder and deacon. Elders have the responsibility of the spiritual oversight of the church; deacons have the responsibility of the practical oversight of the church.

Elders (overseers, bishops, leaders) are the spiritual overseers of God's Church. In Titus we see that elder (1:5) and overseer (1:7) are referring to the same office. The term *elder* gives their basic qualification—older in years and in spiritual maturity. Older is a relative term. If there is a newly planted church of people in their twenties, their elders may be in their late twenties. But what a blessing it is to see grey-haired men of maturity and wisdom, who have walked with God for forty years, functioning as elders.

Overseer tells one thing that the elders are to do—oversee, look over, protect the welfare of the saints and the proper functioning of the Body. *Bishop* is another translation of the same Greek word *episkopos* and was inserted in the King James translation so that the Scriptures would line-up with the practice of the Church of England! The accurate rendering of the word is *overseer*.

In Hebrews 13:7, 17, and 24 we find the word *leader*. This denotes another thing the elders are to do—lead. That does not mean dominate, manipulate, control, or do all of the ministering.

It means lead, go first, set the example. Those in leadership must lay their lives down first and most completely; setting the example in repentance, humility, sacrifice, giving, perseverance, love, joy, righteousness, and peace. Elders are to oversee and lead. The elders also are to teach and to shepherd God's people.[1]

The elders are appointed by apostles. (Yes, there are still apostles today. See Chapter 13.) In Acts 14:23, we see the apostles, Paul and Barnabas, appointing elders in every church which they had planted. They did not appoint a *pastor*, nor did they bring someone in from the outside to oversee the flock. They appointed the most mature of the new believers to be the elders.

The traditional teaching is that Paul instructed Timothy to remain at Ephesus and left Titus at Crete[2] to be the *pastors* of those city churches. This is not our understanding. Apostles evangelize, plant churches, give foundational teaching, appoint elders, and move on. Paul had evangelized and planted churches in these two situations, but did not have time to sufficiently give the foundational teaching and to appoint elders. He left Timothy and Titus, his apostolic associates, behind to complete the foundation-laying process by finishing the foundational teaching and appointing elders. Then they, too, moved on.[3]

The elders in the New Testament were appointed and functioned in plurality. They submitted to one another and worked as a team. The one-man leader type that we see in today's Church and para-church movements is not God's plan for His Church. We do see Philip, the

91

evangelist, sometimes functioning alone. And we see Agabus the prophet sometimes traveling by himself. But all other ministries in the New Testament are seen ministering together in teams. And especially the elders, given to the local oversight of the flock, are appointed in plurality.

One of the qualities that should characterize the individual believer, and the Christian Church collectively, is humility. It is God's plan for His leaders to set the example—walking together with one another in mutual-submission-humility and unity, seeking God together, hearing from Him together, and walking in unity.

The qualifications for elders are given in 1 Timothy 3:1-7, Titus 1:5-9, and 1 Peter 5:2-3. They are primarily personal character traits. Very few people live up to these qualifications all the time, but they should be a pretty consistent part of one's life before he is appointed an elder (or deacon). Generally, the elders are *working* people, although sometimes they may become *full-time*, and receive their support from the saints.[4] (More on the subject of support in Chapter 17.)

Today we have a practice we call *ordination*, and after *being ordained* you are called *Reverend*. The King James translation of Acts 14:23 says, *"And when they had ordained them elders. . ."* This is the Greek word *cheirotoneo*, and means *to vote by stretching the hand, to appoint*. Vine states, ". . . the recognition of those who had been manifesting themselves as gifted of God to discharge the function of elders."[5]

In Titus 1:5, we read, *". . . I left you in Crete, that you might set in order what remains, and appoint elders in every city. . ."* Here *appoint* is the Greek word *kathistemi,* and means *to set in order, appoint.* Vine's comments on this passage are, "Not a formal ecclesiastical ordination is in view, but the appointment, for the recognition of the churches, of those who had already been raised up and qualified by the Holy Spirit, and had given evidence of this in their life and service."[6]

This appointing or recognizing of elders was not some ceremony or rite which put people in a special clergy category. The apostles simply recognized those whom the Lord had raised up to oversee the flock. These elders were ordinary people, who met spiritual qualifications;[7] were raised up by the Holy Spirit; and were recognized and appointed by the apostles to oversee the proper functioning of the Body.[8]

Elders have the spiritual oversight—making sure that the body functions properly, that each individual is released into his or her ministry, that Jesus is Lord, that the Holy Spirit is free to move; encouraging the saints to seek God, to look to Jesus, to be filled and led by the Holy Spirit. To verify all of this teaching on elders, you are encouraged to study Acts 14:23, 20:17-35; Philippians 1:1; 1 Timothy 3:1-7, 5:17-20; Titus 1:5-9; and 1 Peter 5:1-5.

Deacons

Elders have the spiritual oversight. Deacons have the practical oversight. The word *deacon* is from the Greek word *diakonos,* and means *one who executes the commands of another; a servant, attendant, minister.*[9] All Christians are to be servants, as we looked at in Chapter 9. But there

93

are also those who are officially set apart for a particular ministry of serving.[10] It would seem from Acts 6 that the deacons are involved in both the process of serving the practical needs of the body (*"serve tables"* – verse 2); and in coordinating the serving (*"put in charge"* – verse 3).

Deacons might be involved in coordinating such matters as collections, charity, giving to missions, helping the widows, and the practical needs of the saints. Although the word *deacon* is not found in Acts 6:1-6, it would seem that this was the first functioning of this office, overseeing the proper distribution of food to the Greek-Jewish and Palestinian-Jewish widows. The qualifications for deacons is found in Acts 6:3, 5, and 1 Timothy 3:8-13. It would seem from Acts 6:3-6 that deacons should be selected by the congregation and confirmed and prayed over by apostles.

Women in Leadership

Women should be full, functioning members of the Body, as we have tried to state in Chapter 11. And, as you will also see in that chapter, there is credence for females functioning in the anointing of apostle, prophet, evangelist, shepherd, and teacher. But what about women elders and deacons?

Leadership in both the Old and New Testaments was primarily male, as we have already noted in Chapter 11. 1 Timothy 3:1-7 is written in the context of male overseers, i.e., *"the husband of one wife"*; but the passage does not state that elders must be male. 1 Timothy 5:1-2 and

94

Titus 2:2-5 may be talking about *older* men and women. Or these passages may be referring to *elders*, which would make room for female elders. Several writings in the early Church indicate that there was an office of female elders until it was eliminated in A.D. 363 at the Council of Laodicea.[11] About A.D. 200, Tertullian, one of the early Church apologists, wrote that there were four orders of female church officers: deacons, widows, elders, and presiding officers.[12]

As to female deacons, we see that Phoebe was a deacon of the church at Cenchrea.[13] Romans 16:2 refers to Phoebe as *"a helper of many"* (NASB). The Greek word, translated *helper*, is *prostatis*, and means *a woman set over others, a female guardian, protectress, patroness; caring for the affairs of others and aiding them with her resources.* The verb form *proistemi* means *to put before, set over, rule, have charge over, lead, manage, protect, superintend, preside over.*[14] It is the same word that is used in 1 Timothy 5:17 to refer to elders—*"the elders who <u>rule</u> well."* Phoebe was more than a helper; she was a person of authority and responsibility. Among other responsibilities, she was entrusted with carrying Paul's letter to the church at Rome.[15]

1 Timothy 3:11 may be referring to female deacons, the wives of male deacons, females who assisted male deacons, or maybe even female elders. There are several early writings referring to female deacons.[16]

So, perhaps we should not be too dogmatic that there can not be female elders and deacons. Nor should we insist that there has to be. This writer would understand that in God's plan there can be women elders and deacons.[17]

Leaders of the City

The elders and deacons who were appointed in *The Acts* were appointed to function as elders and deacons of the church of that city. Today we have taken the practice of appointing elders and deacons and applied it to our own particular group, be that a church that meets in a building or in a home. These smaller parts of the church of the city do need leadership. It may not be inappropriate to appoint elders and deacons who would function in a particular group, if there are those who qualify, and if the Holy Spirit so leads. However, they should be seen as elders and deacons of the church of that city, not Baptist, Methodist, or house church elders and deacons.

Chapter 12 Notes

1. 1 Timothy 5:17; Acts 20:28; 1 Peter 5:1-4
2. 1 Timothy 1:3; Titus 1:5
3. This is the opinion of this writer. It is substantiated in *Biblical Eldership*, by Alexander Strauch, Lewis & Roth Publishers, P.O. Box 569, Littleton, Colorado 80160, 1986. He states, ". . . Titus was Paul's special <u>temporary</u> representative (Titus 3:12), and not the bishop of Crete as later tradition would have us believe," p. 169.
4. 1 Timothy 5:17-18
5. *Vine's Expository Dictionary of Old and New Testament Words*, W.E. Vine, Fleming H. Revell, Old Tappan, New Jersey, 1981, p. 69.
6. *Vine's*, p. 67.
7. 1 Timothy 3:1-7; Titus 1:5-9
8. Interesting insight into appointing leaders versus this procedure called *ordination* is found in *A Response to the Danvers Statement*, by R.K. McGregor Wright, Christians for Biblical Equality, 380 Lafayette Road S., Suite 122, St. Paul, Minnesota 55107-1216, 1989, pp. 5-8.
9. *Thayer's Lexicon*, no. 1249.
10. Acts 6:1-6; Philippians 1:1; 1 Timothy 3:8, 12
11. This can be verified by checking the following: *God's Word to Women*, by Katherine C. Bushnell, published by Ray B. Munson, P.O. Box 417, North Collins, New York 14111, lesson #32; *A Response to the Danvers Statement*, by R.K. McGregor Wright, Christians for Biblical Equality, St. Paul, Minnesota 55107, 1989, p. 11; and *Women Elders. . . Sinners or Servants?*, by Richard and Catherine Kroeger, Council on Women and the Church, The United Presbyterian

Church in the U.S.A., 475 Riverside Drive, New York, NY 10027, 1981, p. 11.

12. *Will the Real Heretics Please Stand Up*, by David W. Bercot, Scroll Publishing Company, Tyler, Texas 75706, 1989, pp. 19-20; and Kroegers, pp. 9-10.

13. Romans 16:1

14. *NASB Concordance* and *Thayer's*, no. 4368.

15. So state most commentaries and New Testament survey books, based on Romans 16:1-2.

16. These writings include *Phiny's Letter to Emperor Trajan*, dated A.D. 112, mentioned in *The New Testament Deacon*, by Alexander Strauch, Lewis & Roth Publishers, P.O. Box 569, Littleton, Colorado 80160, 1992, p. 177; and *Apostolic Constitutions*, dated around A.D. 380, mentioned in the same book, p. 179.

17. We recommend two publications for further study on the subject of women in Church leadership in the New Testament: the previously mentioned booklet by Kroegers, *Women Elders. . . Sinners or Servants?*; and Wright's *A Response to the Danvers Statement*, especially Part II.

13 Ministries –
Apostles, Prophets, Evangelists, Shepherds, and Teachers

"And He gave some as apostles, and some as prophets, and some as evangelists, and some as pastors and teachers, for the equipping of the saints. . ."   *–Ephesians 4:11-12*

The risen Christ has given, as gifts to His Church, people (male and female) whom He has chosen and gifted as apostles, prophets, evangelists, shepherds, and teachers—

> Therefore it says, "When He ascended on high, He led captive a host of captives, And He gave gifts to men. . . And He gave some (as) apostles, and some (as) prophets, and some (as) evangelists, and some (as) pastors and teachers" (Ephesians 4:8,11).

The purpose of these gifted-ones is to equip God's people for their various ministries (Ephesians 4:12). As a result of all of God's people coming into their various ministries, the church will:
- come into a common faith (4:13)
- come into a full understanding of Jesus (verse 13)

- come to complete maturity, commensurate with the fullness of Christ (verse 13)

- no longer be swayed by every new thing that comes along (verse 14)

- always speak the truth in love (verse 15)

- grow up in all aspects/respects into Jesus (verse 15)

- function as a Body that builds itself up in love (verse 16)

These gifted ones are not a special clergy class. The word *clergy* is nowhere to be found in the Scriptures.[1] They are ordinary believers, part of the Body, whom Jesus has gifted in a particular way as an apostle, prophet, evangelist, shepherd, or teacher. **They are not to do all of the ministering.** They are to walk in humility and servanthood with the rest of the Body. **They are to be coaches; releasing, encouraging, and serving all others in their various ministries.**

Apostles

Apostles are the visionary-pioneers. They are men and women of much vision and faith. They are always pioneering, starting, giving birth to new vision, new churches, new ministries, and new projects. The word *apostle* means *sent one.*[2] They are sent by Jesus to do His will. They are usually involved in evangelism and planting churches, especially where the church does not exist.[3] Their ministry is accompanied by signs and wonders.[4] They live by faith, relying on God's provision, which is often through His people, or they live by their own labors.[5] They live a life of sacrifice and persecution.[6] They persevere when others quit.[7] Their ministry is often behind the scenes, hidden, unknown.[8] They live a life of death to self.[9]

There were the original Twelve apostles. Whether Matthias or Paul took Judas' place is debatable. Some see Matthias,[10] while others see Paul as God's choice, due to Paul's prominence in Scripture. The names of the Twelve will be on the twelve foundation stones of the wall of the new Jerusalem.[11]

Additionally, there is the ministry of the apostle throughout the entire Church Age. Any new entity (vision, church, ministry) has a foundation that is laid by apostles and prophets working together.[12] Those in the New Testament, in addition to the original Twelve, who were gifted by God to be apostles, were Matthias (Acts 1:16); Paul (Romans 1:1, etc.); Andronicas, Junia, others (Romans 16:7); brethren (2 Corinthians 8:23); James, the Lord's brother (Galatians 1:19); Silvanus (Silas) and Timothy (1 Thessalonians 1:1, with 2:6); Barnabas (Acts 14:4, 14); a number (1 Corinthians 15:7, with 15:5); Apollos and Sosthenes (1 Corinthians 4:9, with 1:1 and 4:6); Epaphroditus (Philippians 2:25); and Titus (clearly seen by what he did).

Paul is our primary example in Scripture of an apostle. *The Acts* tells of Peter's travels in chapters 8-11; Barnabas' in 11:22-26, 29-30; and the travels of Paul, Barnabas, and others who worked with them in chapters 13-28.

Paul and Barnabas started out in the setting of the church of Antioch. As they were waiting upon the Lord, the Holy Spirit said that they were to be *set apart* for a new *work*. They were *sent out* by the Holy Spirit and the Antioch church. Once *sent out* they were accountable to the Lord, not to the Antioch church.[13] But they were deeply committed to relationships and fellowshipped and shared with the Antioch brethren whenever they were in Antioch.[14] The apostles submitted themselves to one another for mutual correction.[15]

Some apostles today travel much, like Paul did. Other apostles are located more in one area, like James at Jerusalem and John at Ephesus were. Apostles are able to function as prophet, evangelist, shepherd, and teacher, until such time as God brings these gifts along. Then the apostle pulls back and encourages the others in their area of ministry.

Prophets

Prophets are God's gifted ones with *a word* for the Church. Agabus is our primary example of a New Testament prophet. We see Agabus and others coming from Jerusalem to Antioch to tell of a coming famine.[16] We find prophets functioning in the church at Antioch.[17] We see Judas and Silas chosen to accompany Paul and Barnabas to Antioch.[18] While there, they had a message of encouragement for the church.[19] We read of Agabus coming to Caesarea with a word for Paul.[20]

The Church is to be a prophetic voice to society, and prophets are to lead the Church in Her prophetic ministry. So, it would seem that the prophets also have a prophetic ministry to the world. This was certainly true of the Old Testament prophets who spoke God's Word to kings and nations. The prophets' ministry to the world does not seem to be as clear in the New Testament as it is in the Old.

So prophets have *a word* for the Church—and possibly for the world. Sometimes they are resident; sometimes they are traveling. Sometimes they are alone, sometimes as a team of prophets, sometimes with apostles. They are sometimes sent out by the church[21] and sometimes sent directly by the Spirit Himself.[22]

Evangelists

Philip is our example of an evangelist. He was first chosen to be part of the Seven, to take care of food distribution.[23] When persecution came to the believers at Jerusalem, he went to the city of Samaria.[24] There he preached the Good News about the Christ, cast out demons, and healed the sick.[25] Many believed and were baptized.[26] For a time, the apostles Peter and John came to work with him.[27] Then he was directed by an angel to go to Gaza where he preached Christ to the Ethiopian eunuch.[28] After that he was transported by the Spirit to Azotus, where he preached in all the cities until he came to Caesarea.[29] And, finally, we see Philip at his home in Caesarea, with his four daughters, where he is known as an *evangelist*.[30]

From all of this we can conclude that an evangelist is one gifted by God to preach the Gospel to individuals and to the crowds, to heal the sick, and to cast out demons, wherever God sends him. His ministry is to the unsaved. Because the gifted-ones are to *perfect the saints* for their ministry, the evangelist is also used by to mobilize Christians for witnessing and evangelism.

Shepherds

The words *pastor* and *shepherd* are translated from the Greek word *poimen*.[31] This word occurs eighteen times in the New Testament. Ten of these are referring to Jesus as our Shepherd. When referring to a function in the church it appears only once in the noun form, in Ephesians 4:11, "*And He gave some. . . as pastors.*" Twice we have the verb form—in Acts 20:28, Paul admonished the Ephesian elders (overseers) to "*shepherd the church of God.*" And in 1 Peter 5:1-2, we, likewise, find Peter exhorting the elders to "*shepherd the flock of God among you.*"

We don't have any clear example given in the New Testament of a person functioning in the shepherd ministry. How strange—the one ministry that the New Testament says the least about is the one we hear people talking the most about today. There is such an overuse of the word *pastor*. In some circles anyone in full-time Christian ministry is called *pastor*.

It would appear that shepherds are those men and women, gifted by the risen Christ, to lead, feed, protect, and encourage God's people. They may function as elders in the local church of a city. Not all elders are shepherds. One might be an elder by appointment and function as a prophet or teacher by gifting. And not all shepherds are elders. One might have the gifting of a shepherd and be functioning in that gifting, but not yet have been recognized as an elder. (See Chapter 12 for more on elders.)

Teachers

The teacher is mentioned in Acts 13:1; 1 Corinthians 12:28-29; 1 Timothy 2:7; and 2 Timothy 1:11. The teacher is one given by Jesus to the Church to unfold the meaning of the Scriptures. He is a researcher, always studying, often knows the original Hebrew and Greek, and is able to unfold the purposes of God as written in the Scriptures. He is concerned with the accurate understanding of truth. Sometimes he travels[32] and sometimes he resides in one location.[33]

The apostles, prophets, evangelists, shepherds, and teachers should look to God for their provision. But God usually provides through His people, so God's people need to be sensitive and obedient to the Spirit in their giving. (More on finances in Chapter 17.)

Chapter 13 Notes

1. The word *clergy* probably comes from the Greek word *kleros*, which means *a lot, allotted to your charge, inheritance, portion.* It is used in 1 Peter 5:3, *"those allotted to your charge,"* to refer to those believers whom the elders were to shepherd. A far cry from a special ruling class!

2. The word *missionary*, frequently used today but not found in the Bible, comes from the Latin and also means *sent one.*

3. Romans 15:20

4. Romans 15:19; 2 Corinthians 12:12

5. Philippians 4:15-19; Acts 18:2-3; 1 Corinthians 4:12; 1 Thessalonians 2:9

6. 2 Corinthians 4:5-12, 6:3-10, 11:23-27

7. 2 Corinthians 12:12

8. 2 Corinthians 6:9, 12:11

9. 2 Corinthians 4:5-12

10. Acts 1:15-26

11. Revelation 21:14

12. Ephesians 2:19-22

13. Acts 13:1-3

14. Acts 14:26-28

15. Galatians 2:1-2

16. Acts 11:27-28

17. Acts 13:1

18. Acts 15:22-35

19. Acts 15:32

20. Acts 21:10-11

21. Acts 15:22

22. Acts 21:10-11

23. Acts 6:1-6

24. Acts 8:4-5

25. Acts 8:5-7

26. Acts 8:5-12

27. Acts 8:14-25
28. Acts 8:26-39
29. Acts 8:40
30. Acts 21:8-9
31. *New American Standard Exhaustive Concordance of the Bible*, Robert L. Thomas, General Editor, Holman Publishers, Nashville, Tennessee, 1981, no. 4166.
32. 1 Timothy 2:7; 2 Timothy 1:11
33. Acts 13:1

14 | Church Growth

*"Behold, I say to you, lift up your eyes, and look
on the fields, that they are white for harvest."*

–John 4:35

Jesus has given to His Church a Commission,
to go into all the world and proclaim the
Good News of His Kingdom to every person in
every language, people group, and nation.[1]
Today, after almost 2000 years, there are still
millions, in thousands of people groups, who
have never heard. **How can we see this Great
Commission fulfilled in this generation? By
simply returning to the principles and patterns
of church growth which we see in the New
Testament.**

Everybody, Everywhere, Every Day Witnessing

Every day Jesus was touching lives and
society everywhere He went. The Early Church
naturally followed His simple pattern. They, too,
were touching lives everywhere they went;[2]
every day;[3] as led by the Holy Spirit; as a normal,
natural part of their daily life. We, too, today
need to return to this simple principle and

pattern—every believer;[4] witnessing,[5] loving and serving people,[6] and being a prophetic voice[7] everywhere he goes;[8] every day;[9] as led by the Holy Spirit.[10]

Evangelists

Another aspect of the outreach of the early Church was the work of evangelists. Philip is our example. Everywhere he went he was proclaiming the Good News of the Kingdom to crowds[11] and individuals.[12] His evangelism included casting out demons and healing the sick.[13] So, today, we need to believe God to raise up in our midst thousands of Spirit-baptized evangelists who will go throughout the world proclaiming the Good News, accompanied by signs and wonders.

Apostolic, Church-planting Teams

Another dimension of the evangelism of the Early Church was the sending forth of teams of apostles who were evangelizing; planting simple house churches; giving foundational teaching to those churches;[14] and appointing elders to oversee them.[15] Paul, and his associates, is our pattern for all of this.

Likewise, today, we need to see God raise up teams of apostles who will similarly evangelize individuals and the masses; plant fellowships of believers who will simply gather in their homes; give foundational teaching; appoint elders to oversee them; and then move on to other places.

Signs and Wonders

The operating of the Holy Spirit's gifts and the occurrence of *signs and wonders* are an important part of the evangelism of the early Church,[16] and should be a vital part of our church growth today.

Teaching All Things

Proclaiming the Good News, leading people to Jesus, and planting a church are not the final fulfillment of the Great Commission. Jesus also said, ". . . *teaching them to observe all that I commanded you*" (Matthew 28:20). We must follow-up the new believers, disciple them to walk with Jesus, teach them all that the Holy Spirit has taught us, and encourage them to teach others.[17]

Chapter 14 Notes

1. Matthew 28:18-20; Mark 16:14-20; Luke 24:45-49; John 20:21-23; and Acts 1:4-8
2. Matthew 10:7-8; Acts 8:4
3. Acts 5:42
4. Matthew 4:19; John 15:16
5. Acts 1:8
6. Matthew 25; 1 Corinthians 9:19-22
7. Matthew 5:13-14
8. Acts 8:4
9. Acts 5:42
10. Acts 8:29
11. Acts 8:5-25
12. Acts 8:26-40
13. Acts 8:6-8
14. Acts 2:42; Hebrews 6:1-2
15. Acts 14:21-23
16. Acts 2:43, 4:30, 5:12, 6:8, 14:3, 15:12; Romans 15:19; 2 Corinthians 12:12; and Hebrews 2:4
17. Acts 15:36; Colossians 1:28-29; 2 Timothy 2:2

15 | The Church of the City

". . . the church which is at Cenchrea. . ."

–Romans 16:1

The Greek word *ekklesia,* which is translated into the English word *church,* appears in the English New Testament 114 times. Of these, thirty times it refers to all of the believers in a given city, i.e., *"the church in Jerusalem";*[1] *"the church which is at Cenchrea";*[2] *"the church of God which is at Corinth";*[3] *"the church of the Thessalonians";*[4] *"the church in Ephesus."*[5] There were many believers in these cities, some estimate 50,000 in Jerusalem within a year or two. They were meeting in their various homes. Yet they considered themselves the **church** of that city. All through the New Testament we see the clear principle of **one church per one city**.

Today God is bringing this into focus once again.[6] Many are coming to see that in any given town or city there is only one church, i.e., the church of that city. With that understanding comes an openness and desire to reach out to other parts of that one church, getting acquainted, coming into fellowship, and finding ways to flow and work together as **the church of the city**.

If you are part of a group of believers which gathers in a home, or are part of a network of house churches, you still are simply a part of the church of that city, just like all the other believers in your city.

Chapter 15 Notes

1. Acts 8:1
2. Romans 16:1
3. 1 Corinthians 1:2
4. 1 Thessalonians 1:1
5. Revelation 2:1
6. Recent publications on the church-of-the-city concept include: *Churchlife Handbook*, by Frank B. Smith, P.O. Box 3009, Vista, California 92085-3009; *Taking Our Cities for God*, by John Dawson, Creation House, Lake Mary, Florida 32746, 1989; *Taking Your City for Christ*, a 5-page strategy by Nate Krupp, with Dr. Jay Grimstead, available from Preparing the Way Publishers, 2121 Barnes Avenue SE, Salem, Oregon 97306; *The House of the Lord*, by Francis Frangipane, Creation House, Lake Mary, Florida 32746, 1991; and *The Harvest*, by Rick Joyner, Morningstar Publications, Pineville, North Carolina 28134, 1989.

16 | What to do With the Children

"And, fathers, do not provoke your children to anger; but bring them up in the discipline and instruction of the Lord." –Ephesians 6:4

Parents to Disciple Their Own Children

There are three principles which underlie everything pertaining to this subject. The first principle is that **the family is the most important unit of society**, more important than the church or any other entity. We must return to putting the family unit in first place priority.

The second principle is that God has given the responsibility of training and rearing children to their parents,[1] not to some other entity, be it the Sunday School, Junior Church, or some kids club. Let's quit trying to pass it off on some Sunday School teacher or youth worker. **You become the spiritual leader**, discipler, trainer, pace-setter in your family.

This means living the Christian life before your children. This means giving to them the right combination of **love and affection**,[2] **teaching and training**,[3] and **discipline**.[4]

We recommend a daily time of Family Worship, when the entire family gathers together for about thirty minutes of Bible reading, study, or memory; sharing; singing and worship; and prayer. (Our grown children still know some of the Bible verses they memorized as part of our family worship when they were growing up.)

Children are Part of the Body

The third principle is that the children are part of the Body. Jesus had a great love for children.[5] He demonstrated that there is much that we can learn from them.[6] Nowhere in Scripture do we see them ushered off to some other activity, i.e., Junior Church.

This means that when the church gathers, the children should be part of the gathering. We know of some groups that purposely direct part of the gathering toward the children. They let them pick out songs to sing, and/or they have a brief teaching directed to them. And, of course, they should be allowed to participate in the gathering[7] just like everyone else. Some of the most precious, insightful words that have been shared in some of the gatherings this writer has been in have come spontaneously from the children—real words of wisdom and knowledge, prophetic words, teaching, exhortations, *the word of the Lord*.

If the gathering gets too lengthy, the parents can excuse their children to go to another room or outside. Sometimes, the Holy Spirit leads someone to have something prepared to do with the children once they are excused.

Someone may be led to open their family room or garage for a weekly or monthly youth gathering. There is no limit as to what can be done, as the Holy Spirit is allowed to lead. So listen to Him; get His plan. It will be wonderful.

So include the children in the gatherings of the church. And allow the Holy Spirit to lead in any variety of youth activities. But, remember, these are supplemental to the primary place of training—the home.

Chapter 16 Notes

1. Ephesians 6:4; 1 Timothy 3:4-5; Titus 1:6
2. Colossians 3:21; Titus 2:4
3. Deuteronomy 4:9; Proverbs 22:6; Ephesians 6:4
4. Proverbs 13:24, 19:18, 22:15, 23:13-14, 29:15, 17
5. Mark 9:36-37, 10:13-16
6. Matthew 18:1-4
7. 1 Corinthians 14:26

17|Finances

"Now this (I say), he who sows sparingly shall also reap sparingly; and he who sows bountifully shall also reap bountifully." —2 Corinthians 9:6

We now come to an important and controversial subject—money. Some Christian ministers can't seem to open their mouths without talking about it. Many believers and unbelievers are totally turned off, and many have just plain quit giving. On the other hand, some believers are in real bondage, almost with a sense that their relationship with God depends upon their *paying their tithe.* So what is God's will on all of this? The Bible has much to say about finances and giving. Let's take a look.

Basic Principles of Finances

We will begin by taking a look at some basic principles of finances as spelled out in the Scriptures. This will be presented in outline form, giving Scripture references for you to look up and study on your own, so that you can come to your own conclusions.

1. The whole matter of finances, possessions, and giving will not find its proper place in your life until you **put God first** – Matthew 6:19-34.

2. Then we need to come to the place where **money and possessions** are not our love and **have no hold on us** – Matthew 19:23-24; Mark 4:19, 14:10-11; Luke 12:15-21, 14:16-19, 16:14; Acts 5:1-10, 16:19; Ephesians 5:3; Colossians 3:5-6; 1 Timothy 3:3, 6:10-11; Hebrews 13:5; James 5:1-6.

3. We should be **committed to working** – Genesis 3:17-19; Acts 18:3; Ephesians 4:28; 1 Thessalonians 4:11-12; 2 Thessalonians 3:6-15.

4. We should **not charge for service (ministry) done in Jesus' Name** – Matthew 10:8-9; Luke 10:29-37.

5. We should **be content** with what we have – Philippians 4:11-13; 1 Timothy 6:8; Hebrews 13:5.

6. We should **not go into debt** to acquire more – Deuteronomy 15:6; Romans 13:8.

7. We should **take care of** what we already possess – Ecclesiastes 10:18; Luke 16:10-11.

8. We should have an attitude of having all things in common, desiring to **freely share** what we own with others, even to the extent of bringing others up to our material level – Acts 2:44-45, 4:32-37; 2 Corinthians 8:14; Ephesians 4:28.

9. We should **not go into partnership with the unsaved** – 2 Corinthians 6:14-15.

10. We should be satisfied with God's provision and **not accumulate** beyond our need – Matthew 6:19-34; Luke 12:3-34.

11. We may **loan** to those in need, we need to be patient toward their repayment, and we should not charge interest to a fellow believer – Deuteronomy 23:19-20; Psalms 15:5; Matthew 5:42, 18:21-35; Luke 6:35.

12. We should **not be partial** toward the rich –
James 2:1-6.

13. We should **be honest** in all of our dealings
– Proverbs 11:1, 16:8; Luke 3:13, 19:8; Acts 5:1-10.

14. If we are **defrauded** in any way, we should
not try to regain our just due – Matthew 5:39-42;
Luke 6:29-30; 1 Corinthians 6:7.

15. We are responsible before God for the **total
stewardship** of our lives—time, talents,
possessions, everything – Matthew 25:14-30; Luke
16:10-12; Romans 12:1-2, 14:12; 1 Corinthians 4:2.

16. The practice of tithing is being increasingly
questioned by many.[1] **Tithing** was part of the
Old Covenant but **is not** taught in the New
Testament **as part of the New Covenant.**[2] One is
not required to give ten percent. **He is given the
joyful privilege of giving everything** (total
stewardship) **as the Holy Spirit leads.** We will
see more on this in the next section.

Principles of Giving

Once one is operating by the general
principles of finances listed above, he is then
ready to enter into a joyful life of giving
according to the following principles:

1. **Give yourself first.** Many people give
financially out of pressure and miss the whole
point and joy. We must **first give ourselves**—to
God and to His use of us in the lives of others—
then He will lead us to serve and give as He
wills, not as we will – Matthew 7:21; Mark 8:35;
2 Corinthians 8:1-5.

2. It is **more blessed to give than to receive** –
Acts 20:35.

3. You are privileged and blessed to **give in proportion to how God has financially blessed you** – Luke 12:42-48; Acts 11:29; 1 Corinthians 16:1; 2 Corinthians 8:3, 12.

4. Give **voluntarily** and **cheerfully** – 2 Corinthians 8:3, 9:7.

5. Give **secretly** – Matthew 6:2-4. (We question the present-day practice of *passing the plate*.)

6. Give **systematically** – 1 Corinthians 16:2.

7. **Give to people**, not *bricks*. All of the giving in the New Testament was to people, not to buildings. Today, much of God's people's money goes into buildings. Scripturally, our giving should be to people, as the Holy Spirit directs, in the following categories:

a. Traveling workers – 1 Corinthians 9:6-14; Philippians 4:14-16.

b. Local elders, who are giving themselves full-time to ministry – 1 Timothy 5:17-18.

c. Widows, who have been approved for support, so that they can give themselves to prayer – 1 Timothy 5:3-16.

d. Believers in need – Acts 2:44-45, 4:31-37; Galatians 6:10; 1 Corinthians 16:1; 1 John 3:17-18.

e. The poor – Matthew 25:34-46; Luke 14:12-14; Galatians 2:10.

Why is it today that so many of us would rather give to an organization, a corporate entity, or a building program rather than to an individual person?!

8. There are those who have **the gift of giving**. God has gifted them to make money and give it wisely to the work of God – Romans 12:4-8; 1 Peter 4:10.

9. God leads some people to **part with everything they have** – Matthew 19:21; Mark 12:41-44; Luke 21:1-4; 1 Corinthians 13:3.

10. You will **receive back in proportion** to what you give – Matthew 6:20, 19:21; Luke 6:38, 14:12-14; 2 Corinthians 9:6; Philippians 4:17, 19; 1 Timothy 6:19.

11. **You can't out-give God!** – Mark 19:29-30.

May God bless you as you begin to live according to His financial principles and begin to give voluntarily, joyfully, according to His principles, as the Holy Spirit directs.

Chapter 17 Notes

1. Helpful, confirming input on this was received from *How and Why Do We Give*, by Stephen T. Sherer, in the Revelationship Newsletter, Summer/Fall 1992, P.O. Box 4782, Boise, Idaho 83711-4782.

2. Tithing is mentioned only two times in the New Testament. In Matthew 23:23 (and the parallel passage, Luke 11:42) Jesus is condemning the Pharisees for being so obsessed with tithing rather than the matters which are really important—justice, mercy, faithfulness, and the love of God. He concludes by saying that they shouldn't neglect the tithing. In so doing, He was encouraging them to walk in the light they had, which included tithing. The other place that tithing is mentioned is Hebrews 7:1-9. Here the writer of Hebrews is talking about Abraham giving a tenth to Melchizedek and how the Law required the people to give a tenth to the sons of Levi. This was all part of the Old Covenant. But nowhere in the New Testament is tithing taught as something which should be practiced under the New Covenant. Much of 2 Corinthians is on the subject of money, but not one word is said about tithing.

18 | Church Discipline

". . . If a man is caught in any trespass, you who are spiritual, restore such a one in a spirit of gentleness. . ." —Galatians 6:1

This is not a pleasant subject but one that must be briefly looked at, because it is in the Word of God, and the practice is sometimes necessary. Church discipline falls into three main categories: dealing with problems which arise during *the church gathered*, dealing with those in the church who are living in sin, and dealing with those who are false teachers.

Dealing with Problems Which Arise During *the Church Gathered*

The main problem which might arise during our times of gathering would be when someone tends to monopolize the time—doing too much teaching, too much talking, or too much asking of questions. If the situation isn't dealt with, the gatherings may degenerate into a one-person-centered type of meeting and the Holy Spirit's purposes be quenched. If the correction is done too harshly, the timid or immature in the group will be reluctant to say anything in the future.

The elders need to use great wisdom and gentleness in correcting the situation. We suggest that the elders attempt to talk privately with the individual, explaining the importance of waiting upon the Lord, being careful to be led by the Holy Spirit, not to monopolize, and to give room for all to share. If the situation must be dealt with publicly, it should be done with great love and gentleness.

Dealing with Those in the Church Who are Living in Sin

If we see a fellow Christian clearly living in sin, which might be a sin against you, or might be sin in his life (not just doing something that we may not agree with!), after much prayer, we should go to him and attempt to talk to him about his bondage.[1] If he is not able to understand what you are saying, or not able to agree with what you are saying, then, again after much prayer, you should take two or three others who could bring further clarity and perspective on the matter. If the person is clearly in sin, as unanimously testified to by the several witnesses, and he or she is not willing to see it and to repent, then it needs to be brought to the whole church. If he will not listen to the church, then he should be treated as an unbeliever. When he does repent, he should, of course, with much love and acceptance, be welcomed back into the fellowship. All of this should be conducted in a spirit of great gentleness for the sake of the erring brother.[2] And, if he does repent, and then sins again, we must continue to forgive and receive, as long as he continues to repent, even seven times a day![3]

We should not personally fellowship with, or allow into our fellowship gatherings, anyone who claims to be a believer but is immoral, covetous, idolater, reviler, drunkard, or swindler.[4]

If there are those in your midst who will not work, they should be disfellowshipped for a season until they repent, and yet still regarded as a brother.[5]

There are some who continue in sin who must be turned over to Satan, to experience some of his harsh ways in order to bring them to repentance.[6] This process of turning one over to Satan should not be done by just any believer, but by those in spiritual authority in the situation, either apostles or elders.

Sin must be dealt with, but in a humble, restorative manner, always seeking the good of the offended brother, as well as the good of those who have been offended, and the general life of the church. It takes great love, patience, and wisdom from above!

Dealing with Those Who Teach Contrary to God's Word

If anyone's teaching is divisive, selfish, and flattering, we should turn away from them.[7]

Paul's second letter to Timothy tells us that

> . . . in the last days. . . men will be lovers of self, lovers of money, boastful, arrogant, revilers, disobedient to parents, ungrateful, unholy, unloving, irreconcilable, malicious gossips, without self-control, brutal, haters of

good, treacherous, reckless, conceited, lovers of
pleasure rather than lovers of God; holding to a
form of godliness, although they have denied
its power: (we should) avoid such men as these
(2 Timothy 3:1-5).

There are those who claim to be preaching the
Gospel, but who do not acknowledge that the
Messiah has come in the flesh. We should not
listen to them.[8]

These are just a few guidelines from Scripture
on how to deal with church problems—during
the church gatherings, those in sin, and false
teachers.

Chapter 18 Notes

1. Matthew 18:15
2. Galatians 6:1
3. Luke 17:3-4
4. 1 Corinthians 5:9-13
5. 2 Thessalonians 3:6-15
6. 1 Timothy 1:18-20
7. Romans 16:17-18
8. 2 John 7:11

19 | Common Practices

"For I gave you an example that you also should do as I did to you."   *–John 13:15*

There are six common practices of the Church which we want to take a look at in this chapter: water baptism, the Lord's Supper, foot washing, the love feast, weddings, and funerals. Some would want to make these into some kind of special rite or ordinance which can only be administered by certain people, i.e., *the clergy.* We see them simply as practices common to all believers.

Water Baptism

The English word *baptize* comes from the Greek word *baptizo*, and means *immersion, submersion, or dip.* Baptism is one of the six basic teachings listed in Hebrews 6:1-2. There are five baptisms spoken of in the New Testament. They are:

1. **John's baptism**, which was an immersion into water of one who was repenting of his or her sins, which was later replaced by Christian baptism done in Jesus' Name.[1]

2. Being **baptized**, or placed, **into the Body of Christ**, which God does when one experiences the new birth.[2]

3. **Christian baptism**, being immersed in water in the Name of Jesus, as the beginning point of the Christian life. We will look at this more shortly.

4. The **baptism in the Holy Spirit** is an enduement of power, when one is immersed in the Holy Spirit, that equips the child of God for ministry. We looked at this in Chapters 4 and 10.

5. The **baptism of suffering**[3] is an immersion into suffering, when God allows a person to go through a time of deep trial, tribulation, persecution, suffering for purposes which sometimes only He knows. The Fire purifies + Refines

Christian baptism is the immersing in water of one who has turned from his sins (repented), is placing his faith in Jesus as his Savior, and is surrendering his life to Jesus as Lord. It is the initial step of identification with, and surrender to, Christ; and the step of initiation into a walk with Him, which one takes to begin his Christian life.

Jesus was baptized by John *"to fulfill all righteousness,"* i.e., to do what is right.[4] Jesus and His disciples baptized people.[5] In *The Acts*, all who turned from their sins to Jesus were baptized.[6]

Water baptism is closely associated with salvation;[7] places one into His death and resurrection;[8] is to be followed by a changed life;[9] and is closely associated with the baptism in the Holy Spirit.[10]

People should be baptized as soon as they come to Jesus.[11]   Anyone can baptize another person, and the most natural person to do it is the one that helped them come to know Jesus. The words spoken over the person at the time of their baptism may include some combination of *in the Name of the Father and the Son and the Holy Spirit* and *in* or *into the Name of the Lord Jesus Christ*.[12]

The Lord's Supper

The second common practice which we will look at is the *Lord's Supper*, or *communion*. Jesus began this practice when He broke bread and passed the cup at the end of His Last Supper with the Twelve.[13]   The early Church broke bread from house to house.[14]   It seemed to be an important part of their gatherings.[15]   Paul teaches on the proper practice in 1 Corinthians 10:16-21 and 11:17-34.

Many believers who gather in homes today have communion or the Lord's Supper each week. Some have it less frequently. These groups most commonly have one loaf which is broken in the act of distribution. Many groups still have a common cup, but the AIDS epidemic has caused some groups to go to individual cups or glasses. Some have adopted a practice of allowing people to dip their bread into a common cup. Some groups use wine and others use grape juice, or even some other juice if grape juice is not available.

The Lord's Supper can be a wonderful way to end an evening of fellowship with another couple.

It can be a scriptural finale to a dinner together with your family or friends. In our home, it is the highlight of our time together when our children and grandchildren are able to all come home (about once a year!).

There are so many wonderful ways to express love and fellowship when the bread is passed. One person can break the loaf, go to two others and tell them how much God and/or he loves them. Or he can tell them how much Jesus has done for them. Then each of those two can go to two others, etc. The father (or anyone in the family) can take enough bread to share with each member of the family, with appropriate words to each one. Or one can take enough bread to go to whomever he feels led to go to. So ask the Holy Spirit to lead you in a great variety of ways of remembering Him Who died for us that we might live for Him.

Again, we would not see communion as something which can be served by only a special *clergy* class, but as a wonderful time of remembering Jesus, His death, and His resurrection shared by two or more believers anytime they feel led to partake.

Foot Washing

In *John's Gospel* Jesus washed His disciple's feet as an act of humility and instructed them to do the same.[16] Only a small segment of the Lord's Church today follows this admonition. It can be a very blessed and wonderful time of humbling, asking forgiveness, repentance, and fellowship. When a group of believers does this, men and women are often separated into different rooms, with men washing men's feet and women washing women's feet. Some type of wash basin or dish pan and towel can be provided. We have even heard of *handy-wipes* being used!

Love Feasts

Jude 12 is the only New Testament passage which specifically mentions the *love feast*. The Lord's Supper was first practiced by Jesus in connection with a meal—the Passover Meal. It continued to sometimes be associated with a meal.[17] It would appear that the Love Feast was a meal sometimes shared together as part of the gathering of the believers. The Lord's Supper often ended the meal.

Today, many home churches have a shared meal as part of their weekly gathering. Many groups gather on Sunday morning for a time of worship, fellowship, teaching, and prayer; and follow this with a shared meal and fellowship together. Some groups only have the meal monthly; others, weekly; others, every other week; and, others, only occasionally as the Holy Spirit directs. This author was part of a group in the 1960s which met on Sunday at noon for a fellowship meal together, followed by an afternoon of worship and teaching. Look to the Holy Spirit for His leading.

Weddings

The Bible talks about weddings.[18] There are a number of references which indicate parental consent, blessing, and release to the couple.[19]

Jesus performed His first miracle while attending a wedding.[20]

Although most of these references are to Jewish weddings, it would not seem to be inappropriate to have Christian weddings. But does this mean that we need to have these huge weddings, officiated by the *clergy*, where thousands of dollars are spent? The Lord might lead one to have a *big* wedding. But it might also be a simple acknowledgement before the saints, at their weekly gathering, by the couple that they believe they are to be husband and wife, with the blessing and prayers of the church, followed by the normal shared meal and Lord's Supper together. You will probably want to follow your local government regulations and procure whatever license is necessary to keep it all legal.[21]

Funerals

The practice of people burying their dead is found in the Scriptures.[22] But, again, why all of the expense and a *service* conducted by the *minister*? Why not a simple burying of the departed one's body, with the gathering of family members and friends to encourage the remaining family members? And, of course, if the departed one is a believer, what a time of rejoicing and celebration it can be—he or she is now with Jesus!

Here are six common practices which the church may find itself involved in from time to time. All are ways to exalt Jesus for Who He is and for what He is doing! Participate with great joy and under the Holy Spirit's leading and blessing.

Chapter 19 Notes

1. Acts 19:3-5
2. 1 Corinthians 12:13
3. Mark 10:38-39; Luke 12:50
4. Matthew 3:13-17; Mark 1:9; Luke 3:21
5. John 3:22, 26, 4:1-2
6. Acts 2:41, 8:12, 8:38, 9:18, 10:48, 16:15, 16:33, 18:8, 19:5, 22:16
7. Mark 16:16; Acts 2:38, 22:16; 1 Peter 3:21
8. Romans 6:1-11; Galatians 3:27; Colossians 2:12
9. Matthew 3:8-10; Luke 3:8-9; Romans 6:4-11
10. Acts 2:38, 8:12-17, 9:17-18, 10:44-48, 19:1-7
11. Acts 2:41, 8:12-13, 8:38, 9:18, 10:47-48, 16:14-15, 16:33, 18:8
12. Matthew 28:19; Acts 2:38, 8:16, 10:48, 19:5
13. Matthew 26:26-30; Mark 14:22-26; Luke 22:19-20
14. Acts 2:42-46
15. Acts 20:7
16. John 13:1-17
17. Acts 2:46; 1 Corinthians 11:17-22
18. Genesis 29:22-23; Psalms 78:63; Song of Solomon 3:11; Matthew 22:2-12, 25:1-13; Luke 12:35-40, 14:7-11; John 2:1-11
19. Genesis 21:21, 34:4-6; Joshua 15:16; Judges 14:2-3; 1 Corinthians 7:37-38
20. John 2:1-11
21. Most will want to follow this procedure. However, there are those *voices in the wilderness* who are encouraging to dispense with the license, since, in their view, this legally binds you with the state and opens the door for the state having authority over your family. For more on this view, you are encouraged to read *Your*

Christian Marriage and What the State Didn't Tell You About It! by Dr. Leonard B. Zike, Embassy of Heaven, 10505 SE 85th, Portland, Oregon 97266.
   22. Genesis 23, 47:29-30, 49:29, 50:5-14, etc., in the Old Testament; and Matthew 8:21-22, Luke 9:59-60, and Acts 5:6-10 in the New Testament.

20 | Questions Answered

"Now concerning the things about which you wrote. . ."
                                    –1 Corinthians 7:1

What Should We Call Ourselves?

One of the first things most Christian groups do is to give themselves a name: First Christian Church, Men With Vision, Reaching Children, etc. But why do we do this? Usually it is to bring attention to ourselves, that we are distinct in some way from other groups. Taking a name divides the Body; you are either part of that group or you are not. Jesus came to initiate *one new man*,[1] not 20,000 denominations. (That's right, there are over 20,000 denominations around the world plus thousands of independent groups and para-church groups.) Why are we not content to just be followers of Jesus doing whatever He has told us to do? We encourage you not to take a name. Be content to just have His Name! Be content to just be a child of God, a follower of Jesus. Fellowship with all believers. Work with all believers with whom the Lord links you.

What About Incorporating?

Most Christian groups think that they must incorporate in order to be legitimate. We disagree. Jesus said, *"Render to Caesar the things that are Caesar's, and to God the things that are God's"* (Mark 12:17). There are areas of our lives into which government (Caesar) has a right to be involved: our obeying legitimate laws and our paying legitimate taxes. But our religious life is not the concern of the government. It is between God and us. When you incorporate, you give the government legal right into your religious affairs. It is none of their business! And, remember, government blessing today usually means government control tomorrow.[2] We encourage you not to incorporate. Be content to be just a group of believers doing whatever Jesus is showing you to do to obey and exalt Him.[3]

What About a Statement of Faith?

Most Christian groups find it necessary to have a list of their beliefs, usually called a Statement of Faith. But such a Statement usually brings division to the Body. It usually makes an issue out of some doctrine, i.e., is the rapture before, during, or after the tribulation?; is speaking in tongues the initial evidence?; etc., etc. It results in some people being able to join that group because they agree with the Statement of Faith and others not feeling comfortable about joining because of something in the Statement that should be added, deleted, or changed. So why have a Statement of Faith?

Our fellowship should not be based upon doctrinal agreement. Jesus has told us as His followers to lay our lives down for one another.[4] We have no alternative but to accept, love, fellowship with, work with, and lay our lives down for all who know and love Jesus Christ.

Therefore, we recommend that you have no Statement of Faith.[5] Whatever home church or church group you are a part of, you are simply believers in Jesus and as such are part of the Church of your city and the world-wide Body of Christ.

What About Membership?

Most Christian groups have a practice called *membership*, when one officially joins the group. We do not find this practice in Scripture. As believers, we are all *"members one of another."*[6]

As with the Name and Statement of Faith, it means that some people are *in* and some are *out* of the group. Jesus wants us to gather with any and all believers, on the basis of the cross alone, at any time and in any place. We encourage you to not have membership.

How Should Decisions Be Made?

Most of us are used to making decisions either by dictatorial rule, i.e., the one *in charge* makes the decision, or by democratic principles, i.e., a vote is taken and the majority rules. But in His Church, God has a different method whereby decisions are to be made. In the church we are to wait upon the Lord, hear His voice, come into unity, and be agreed upon any decision which is to be made.[7]

We have heard of several situations where a group of elders were seeking God about a matter, and were all agreed, except one. They were tempted to proceed, based on *majority rule*. But they were committed to being _in one accord_, so they didn't. As they continued to seek the Lord, they actually all ended up agreeing with the lone brother. God was using him as a check. How important it is to wait!

The other ways might seem easier on the surface, but God's ways are always better in the long run. What a delight it is to walk in unity, hear from Him in unity, and make decisions in unity!

Be more concerned with unity.

Chapter 20 Notes

1. Ephesians 2:13-22

2. It is already illegal in a growing number of cities in America to have home church meetings or even a home Bible study group (information from Citizen's Bar Association, P.O. Box 935, Medford, Oregon 97501). This clearly violates the 1st Amendment of the U.S. Constitution. These ordinances need to be challenged.

3. For further information on not incorporating, you are encouraged to order *State Churches through Incorporation and Taxation*, by Dr. Greg Dixon, The American Coalition of Unregistered Churches, P.O. Box 11 Indianapolis, Indiana 46206; *God, Inc.*, by Jay Ferris, R.R. 2, Bostic, North Carolina 28018; *The Sufficiency of the Scriptures*, by George Geftakys, Torch and Testimony Publications, P.O. Box 5070, Fullerton, California 92838; and *Examining the Evidence*, and other booklets, by Dr. Leonard B. Zike, Embassy of Heaven, 10505 SE 85th, Portland, Oregon 97266.

4. John 13:34-35

5. If you feel you must have a Statement of Faith, keep it simple. Examples would include *Jesus is Lord*, or *The Bible is our guide for all of life.*

6. Romans 12:5

7. Psalms 133; Acts 1:14, 2:46, 4:32, 13:2, 15:25; Romans 12:16, 15:5; Philippians 1:27, 2:1-8

21 | Where Do We Go From Here?

"But Jesus said to him, 'No one, after putting his hand to the plow and looking back, is fit for the kingdom of God.'" —Luke 9:62

You have prayerfully read this book. Some of it you agree with. Some of it you don't agree with. Some of it you're not sure about. So where do you go from here?

1 John 1:5-7 talks about walking in the light. That's the first thing that all of us must do—walk in, i.e., live by all of the truth that we have already received. Then we need to ask God to give us open, teachable minds and hearts. We must be open to learn new things and also open to unlearn some of the things of the past. Then we need to seek God for more light. We need to ask Him to lead us in His path, not in the traditions of men.[1] As we walk in the truth we already have, are open to learn and unlearn, and seek God for more of His ways, He will lead us.

He will show you His plan for His Church as it relates to your life. It may be like this book; it may not. There are many individuals and churches which are clearly in a time of transition.[2] He will show you His path for you. Begin to walk it, regardless of how radical it may seem, and regardless of what others say or do.

Continue to walk the path He lays out for you—don't look back.[3] The greatest, most glorious days lie ahead! He is Lord!

Chapter 21 Notes

1. Matthew 15:1-9; Mark 7:6-9
2. A booklet on fifteen major ways that the Church is in transition today, entitled *New Wine Skins—The Church in Transition*, by Nate Krupp, is available from Preparing the Way Publishers, 2121 Barnes Avenue SE, Salem, Oregon 97306.
3. Luke 9:62

Appendix 1 —
A Bible Study on Important Issues Regarding Our Lord's Church

This Bible Study has been developed on the truths spelled out in this book and can be used to share these truths in a condensed manner with others.

1. Question—Where do we find out God's plan for His Church?

Answer—The Bible, especially the New Testament - 2 Timothy 3:16-17.

2. Question—How is the word *church* (*ekklesia* in Greek) used in the New Testament?

Answer—It never refers to a building, denomination, or organization. It is always talking about the *called out ones*, i.e., the people who have been called out of the world into a relationship with God; or, the *people of God*. We are God's house – 1 Corinthians 3:16-17; Ephesians 2:19-22; 1 Peter 2:5.

3. Question—How many churches are there in a given city?

Answer—Only one, i.e., all the *called out ones* living in that city – Acts 15:4; 1 Corinthians 1:2; 1 Thessalonians 1:1; Revelation 2:1, etc.

4. Question—What is the church to do?

Answer—Love, worship, and obey God – Matthew 22:38-39; John 4:23-24; Acts 13:2; Philippians 3:3. Truly love and minister to one another – Matthew 22:38-39; 1 Thessalonians 5:11; Hebrews 10:24-25. Minister to the needy – Matthew 25:31-46; Galatians 6:10. Fulfill the Great Commission – Mark 16:14-20; Matthew 28:18-20; Acts 1:8.

5. Question—Where is the church to come together?

Answer—After being thrown out of the Temple, the Early Church met in their homes for about three hundred years – Acts 2:46, 12:12; 1 Corinthians 16:19; Colossians 4:15; Philemon 2.

6. Question—When is the church to gather?

Answer—On the first day of the week (Acts 20:7; Revelation 1:10) and anytime (Acts 2:46; Colossians 2:16-23; Romans 14:4-12).

7. Question—What is to happen when the church comes together?

Answer—Activities when the church is together include fellowship, teaching, meals, Lord's Supper, prayer (Acts 2:42), worship and ministry to the Lord (John 4:24; Acts 13:2), Bible reading (1 Timothy 4:13), spiritual gifts operating (1 Corinthians 12-14), fasting (Acts 13:3), dialogue (Acts 20:7), offering taken for specific purposes (1 Corinthians 16:1-3), local leaders appointed (Acts 14:23) and workers sent out (Acts 13:3).

8. Question—With whom should you gather?

Answer—Some combination of those in your geographical area, everyone who loves Jesus, and those with whom God has knit you.

9. Question—Who is to minister when the church is together?

Answer—Anyone (men and women) led by the Spirit to do so – 1 Corinthians 14:26; Ephesians 4:15-16.

10. Question—Who is responsible for the oversight of the church?

Answer—A group called elders – Acts 14:23, 20:17-32; 1 Timothy 3:1-7; Titus 1:5-9; 1 Peter 5:1-5. They are assisted by deacons – Acts 6:1-6; 1 Timothy 3:8-13. The present-day practice of having a *minister* or a *pastor*, who does most of the ministering, has no biblical basis. (Pastor is a function, not a position.)

11. Question—What about tithing/giving?

Answer—Rather than a set amount (10% in the Old Testament), under the New Covenant, God's people are encouraged to live a simple lifestyle that allows them to give generously as the Spirit leads: to the support of full-time elders (1 Timothy 5:17-18); traveling ministries (1 Corinthians 9:6-23; Philippians 4:10-20); needy believers (2 Corinthians 8 and 9); widows (1 Timothy 5:3-16); and the poor (Matthew 25:31-46).

12. Question—Who is to give Christian training to children?

Answer—Their parents – Ephesians 6:4; Deuteronomy 11:19; Proverbs 13:24, 22:6; Psalm 78:3-7.

13. Question—How are decisions to be made by the church?

Answer—In unity – Psalm 133; Acts 1:14, 13:2; Philippians 1:27, 2:1-8. The present-day practice of voting, with the majority being the decision, has no biblical basis.

14. Question—Who is the Leader of the Church?

Answer—Jesus! – Matthew 23:8-12; Ephesians 1:20-23.

15. Question—Are we to follow the Word of God or the traditions of men?

Answer—Matthew 15:1-9; Mark 7:6-9.

Appendix 2 —

A Comparison of Today's Church with the Church of the New Testament

This chart[1] has been prepared in an attempt to compare some aspects of today's Church with the Church as seen functioning in the New Testament. We trust it will challenge all of us to seek God afresh for His will to be done in His Church today.

	Today's Church	The Church of the New Testament
1. Where do we find God's plan for His church?	Church-growth seminars	The New Testament
2. What is the church?	A building	The people of God
3. Where is Jesus?	In heaven	On earth, at work through His Body
4. What known by?	Their name, building, pastor, doctrine, programs	Their love
5. Taught to	Go to church	Be the church
6. Commitment	Enlarge the institution	Enlarge Christ's Kingdom
7. Key task	Come, grow with us	Go, make disciples
8. Expectations of members	Attendance, tithing, work in the programs	Total commitment and stewardship to Jesus
9. How many churches in any city?	Many	One

	Today's Church	The Church of the New Testament
11. Worship	Is a time and place	Is a lifestyle
12. When is the church to gather?	Sunday and mid-week	Anytime
13. Why does the church gather?	Have a service	To experience *koinonia*
14. Where does the church gather?	Church building	Their homes, anywhere
15. Size of groups	Large, impersonal	Small, intimate
16. Focus of gathering	The pastor	The risen Lord
17. Who is to minister when the church gathers?	The pastor	Anyone led by the Spirit to do so
18. Support system	Problem? See the pastor	Building up one another
19. Relationships	Surface	Intimate, in life together
20. Discipling	Classroom	Being together
21. Oversight of the church	The pastor	A group called elders
22. Primary task of leadership	Direct the program	Equip and release people of God to minister
23. Leadership style	Centralization	Decentralization
24. Source for securing workers	Bible school, seminary	God raises them up from within
25. Who is to disciple the children?	Sunday school teachers and youth workers	Their parents
26. Where is evangelism to take place?	The church building	Everywhere
27. Church growth	Requires bigger building	Spontaneous multiplication
28. Publicity	Madison Avenue techniques	Signs and wonders

	Today's Church	The Church of the New Testament
29. How give?	Offering taken	In secret
30. How much are you to give?	10%	100%
31. Where does the money go?	Buildings	Needs of people
32. How are decisions to be made?	Voting, majority rules	In unity
33. Legal status	Given authority to exist by state corporation	No connection with authorities

Appendix 2 Notes

1. Much of this chart is original with the author, but some has been gotten from Dave Block of Colorado Springs, Colorado; from Ralph Neighbour's book *Where Do We Go From Here?*, Touch Publications, Houston, Texas, 1990, p. 58; and *Searching Together*, Box 548, St. Croix Falls, Wisconsin 54024.

Appendix 3 —
Basics of Home Fellowships

Below are the basic essentials of a house church or home fellowship.

1. Supreme goal—to love God with all your heart, and your neighbor as yourself.

2. Keep it simple, natural, reproducible—no name, no corporation, no property, meet in homes.

3. Built on:

   a. the Lordship of Jesus Christ

   b. the Word of God as guide for all of life

   c. God-formed relationship—walking in humility with one another, encouraging one another to walk in the light that each has

   d. Holy Spirit's full role—fullness, fruit, gifts, ministries, leading, freedom

   e. No clergy/laity distinction—open to ministry of all, shared leadership walking in mutual submission

4. Parents giving Christian training to their own children and children being encouraged to participate in the church's gatherings.

5. Protective oversight—apostolic team, then appointed elders.

Additional Recommended Reading

This list has been updated for this second edition.

A History of the Christian Church. Qualben, Lars P. Thomas Nelson, New York, NY 1968. Early chapters give good view of how the Church changed from early, biblical form to later, non-biblical forms.

A Lost Secret of the Early Church. Pethybridge, W.J. Bethany Fellowship, Minneapolis, MN 55438. About home meetings.

Archaeological Evidence of Church Life Before Constantine. Snyder, Graydon F. SeedSowers Publishing, P.O. Box 3317, Jacksonville, FL 32206, 1985. Title gives subject.

Biblical Eldership. Strauch, Alexander. Lewis and Roth Publishers, P.O. Box 569, Littleton, CO 80160, 1988. An eldership form of government rather than a one-man pastor.

Body Life. Stedman, Ray C. Regal Books, 2300 Knoll Drive, Ventura, CA 93003, 1972. An early writing on the Church functioning as a body, not an audience.

Brethren, Hang Loose. Girard, Robert C. Zondervan, Grand Rapids, MI 49506, 1972. One church and their daring commitment of abandonment to the Lordship of Christ.

Building the House Church. Barrett, Lois. Herald Press, Scottdale, PA, 1986. A basic book on the house church concept.

Christian History, Volume 37—Worship in the Early Church. P.O. Box 11631, Des Moines, IA 50340-1631. This particular issue of t his excellent magazine deals entirely with the life of the Church during the first three centuries after Christ.

Christians for Biblical Equality, 380 Lafayette Road S., Suite 122, St. Paul, MN 55107. An excellent source for books with a similar perspective as this author's on God's plan for women.

Church Leadership. Richards, Lawrence O. and Hoeldtke, Clyde. Zondervan, Grand Rapids, MI 40506, 1980. Restructuring the church to provide for Jesus' leadership, the functioning of the Body, and servant leaders.

Church Life Before Constantine. Snyder, Graydon. SeedSowers Publishing, P.O. Box 3317, Jacksonville, FL 32206, 1985. Excellent about the early Church.

Churchlife Handbook. Smith, Frank B. Crushed Grapes Ministry, P.O. Box 3009, Vista, CA 92085-0316. A practical approach to the city-church.

Church Multiplication Guide. Patterson, George. William Carey Library, P.O. Box 40129, Pasadena, CA 91114. The planting and multiplication of indigenous churches.

Church of My Dreams. Beaumont, John. Destiny Image Publishers, Shippensburg, PA 17257. How the church should reflect the character of God.

Church Without Walls. Petersen, Jim. NavPress, Colorado Springs, CO 80935, 1992. Moving the Church beyond traditional boundaries.

Covenant Relationships. Intrater, Keith. Destiny Image Publishers, Shippensburg, PA 17257, 1989. A manual on interpersonal relationships.

DAWN 2000: 7 Million Churches to Go. Montgomery, Jim. William Carey Library, P.O. Box 40129, Pasadena, CA 91114. Completing the Great Commission by saturation church planting.

Every-Member Evangelism. Conant, J.E. Revell, Westwood, NJ, 1922. God's plan for evangelism—everybody, everywhere, every day evangelism.

Foundation for Restoration. Berry, Michael J. Revival Press, Bedford, TX 76021, 1988. A manual on what God is restoring to His Church today.

Going to Church in the First Century. Banks, Robert. SeedSowers Publishing, P.O. Box 3317, Jacksonville, FL 32206, 1980. A look at a gathering of Christians in the First Century.

Going to the Root. Smith, Christian. Herald Press, Scottdale, PA 15683, 1992. Nine proposals for radical Church renewal.

Home Cell Groups and House Churches. Hadaway, DuBose, and Wright. Broadman Press, Nashville, TN, 1987. Title gives subject.

House Churches Among the Churches of Christ During the 1980s. Harp, Verlon. Star Bible Publications, Fort Worth, TX 76118, 1987. About house churches as understood and practiced currently among the Churches of Christ.

House to House: Spiritual Insights for the 21st Century Church. Kreider, Larry. Touch Outreach Ministries, P.O. Box 19888, Houston, TX 77079, 1995.

Houses that Change the World. Simson, Wolfgang. OM Publishing, P.O. Box 1047, Waynesboro, GA 30830. One of the best on the house church paradigm.

How Christianity Grows in the City. Jennings, Alvin. Star Bible Publications, Fort Worth, TX 76118, 1985. Reaching cities through house churches.

Liberating the Laity. Stevens, R. Paul. Inter-Varsity Press, Downers Grove, IL 60515, 1985. Taking seriously the *priesthood of all believers.*

Love Covers. Billheimer, Paul E. Christian Literature Crusade, Fort Washington, PA 19034, 1981. Agape love bringing unity to the Body of Christ.

Meetings in His Kingdom: Jesus Personally Leading His Church. . . in Home, City, and Multi-City Gatherings. Peters, Mike. Kingdom Publishing, P.O. Box 68309, Indianapolis, IN 46268, 1990.

Missionary Methods: St. Paul's or Ours. Allen, Roland. Moody Press, Chicago, IL, 1956. Planting self-governing, self-propagating, self-financing churches—a classic.

New Testament Order. Hay, Alexander R., New Testament Missionary Union, Audubon, NJ, 1947. A classic on the New Testament church.

New Wine Skins. Krupp, Nate. Preparing the Way Publishers, 2121 Barnes Avenue SE, Salem, OR 97306, 1990. Fifteen ways God is changing His Church today.

One Body in Christ. Kurosaki, Kokichi. Banner Publications, Monroeville, PA 15146, 1968. Oneness in Jesus Christ.

Out of the Comfort Zone—the Church in Transition. Hall, Dudley. MorningStar Publications, P.O. Box 369, Pineville, NC 28134, 1991. Today's changing Church.

Paul's Idea of Community. Banks, Robert. Eerdmans, Grand Rapids, MI 49506, 1979. House churches as seen in the New Testament.

Prepared for His Glory. Rumble, Dale. Destiny Image, Shippensburg, PA 17257, 1986. The end-time restoration of the Church.

Restoration in the Church. Virgo, Terry. Kingsway Publications, Eastbourne, E. Sussex, England, 1985. The present-day house church movement in England.

Rethinking the Wineskin: The Practice of the New Testament Church. Viola, Frank. Present Testimony Ministry, 918 Delaney Circle #205, Brandon, FL 33511. Title gives subject.

Scroll Publishing Company, P.O. Box 6175, Tyler, TX 75711. An excellent source for books about the Early Church.

Searching Together. P.O. Box 548, St. Croix Falls, WI 54024. A quarterly magazine on New Testament Christianity.

1700 Years is Long Enough. Rutz, James H. SeedSowers Publishing, P.O. Box 285, Sargent, GA 30275, 1991. The need to get back to the simplicity of the early Church.

Sixteen Tests of an Authentic New Testament Church. Fellowship Bible Church, 886 S. 86th Street, Tacoma, WA 98444. Title gives subject.

Show the House to the House. Sonmore, Clayt E. 12100 Marion Lane, Suite 6104, Minnetonka, MN 55343, 1990. An eleven-volume series giving a thorough presentation of what God has been trying to do since 1948 and how it has been thwarted by much of the organized church.

Spiritual Leadership. Sanders, J. Oswald. Moody Press, Chicago, IL, 1980. Character qualifications for spiritual leaders.

The Believers' Church. Durnbaugh, Donald F. Herald Press, Scottdale, PA 15683, 1968. Churchlife as practiced by the Mennonites and other groups seeking to recover the New Testament norm.

The Called-Out Assembly. Yisrael, Yericho. P.O. Box 1525, Phoenix, AZ 85001, 1990. A very radical book about coming out of the organized churches to be the *called-out Assembly.*

The Church and the Work. Nee, Watchman. Christian Fellowship Publishers, Richmond, VA 23235, 1982. A three-volume series given as messages by Watchman Nee in China in the 1930s. Includes an unedited, more complete presentation of *The Normal Christian Church Life.*

The Church Comes Home. Banks, Robert & Julia. Hendrickson Publishers, Peabody, MA 01961, 1998. Very good on house church concept.

The Church: His Body, His Bride. Thomas Lowe Ltd., P.O. Box 1049, Cathedral Station, New York, NY 10025, 1982. Small booklet giving basics of the New Testament church.

The Church in the New Testament. Conner, Kevin J. Bible Temple Publishing, 7545 Glisan, Portland, OR 97213, 1989. Extensive look at the church in the New Testament.

The Church Triumphant. Krupp, Nate. Destiny Image, Shippensburg, PA 17257, 1988. Now available from PTWP, 2121 Barnes Avenue SE, Salem, OR 97306. The end-time church characterized by revival, restoration, unity, world evangelization, and persecution.

The Church Without Walls. Goslin, Thomas S. Hope Publishing House, P.O. Box 60008, Pasadena, CA 91106, 1984. A network of house churches in Madrid, Spain.

The Complete Wineskin. Eberle, Harold. Winepress Ministries, P.O. Box 10653, Yakima, WA 98909-1653. Jesus' plan for His Church.

The Diakonate. Rumble, Dale. Torbay Publishing Ltd., 29 Milber Industrial Estate, Newton Abbot, Devon, England TQ12 4SG. Home churches and servant leaders.

The Early Christians. Arnold, Eberhard. Plough Publishing House, Rifton, NY, 1970. The early Church from the extra-biblical writings of the early Christians.

The Early Church. Edwards, Gene. SeedSowers Publishing, P.O. Box 3317, Jacksonville, FL 32206, 1974. A portrayal of the early Church in *The Acts* written as a novel.

The Harvest. Joyner, Rick. Morningstar Publications, P.O. Box 369, Pineville, NC 28134, 1989. Preparing the Church for coming harvest and persecution.

The House Church. Birkery, Del. Herald Press, Scottdale, PA 15683, 1988. A good overview on the subject of house-churches.

The House of the Lord. Frangipane, Francis. Creation House, Lake Mary, FL 32746, 1991. It takes a city-wide church to win a city-wide war.

The King and His Kingdom. Whyte, Peter. Successful Christian Living, P.O. Box 1613, Cape Town, 8000, Republic of South Africa. A comparison of the radical Kingdom that Jesus is establishing with today's church.

The Leadership Paradox. Gunderson, Denny. YWAM Publishing, Seattle, WA. Servant leadership.

The Master Plan of Evangelism. Coleman, Robert E. Fleming H. Revell, Old Tappan, NJ 07675, 1963. Jesus' simple, master plan for world evangelization.

The New Reformation. Ogden, Greg. Zondervan, Grand Rapids, MI 49506, 1990. A call to equip the entire church for ministry.

The New Testament Deacon. Strauch, Alexander. Lewis and Roth Publishers, P.O. Box 569, Littleton, CO 80160, 1992. A thorough study of the office of deacon.

The Open Church. Rutz, James H. Open Church Ministries, 333 Reddick Road, Portal, GA 30450, (888)OPEN 1-2-3, 1992. How to change your church to be more like the early Church.

The Paradox of Servant Leadership. Rinehart, Stacy. NavPress, Colorado Springs, CO 80934. Servant leadership.

The Pilgrim Church. Broadbent, E.H. Pickering & Inglis, Ltd., London, England, 1931. The remnant throughout Church history which has never been part of the organized church.

The Problem of Wine Skins. Snyder, Howard. Inter-Varsity Press, Downers Grove, IL 60515, 1975. A call for new wine skins.

The Quiet Revolution. Henley, Gary. Creation House, Carol Stream, IL 60187, 1970. How to have a New Testament church today.

The Sufficiency of the Scriptures. Geftakys, George. Torch and Testimony Publications, P.O. Box 5070, Fullerton, CA 92838, 1986. Especially good on not having a Statement of Faith and not incorporating.

The Team Concept. Stabbert, Bruce. Hegg Brothers Printing, 2933 N. Stevens, Tacoma, WA 98407, 1982. About a leadership team of elders rather than a one-man pastor.

The Torch of the Testimony. Kennedy, John W. Available from The SeedSowers, P.O. Box 3368, Auburn, ME 04212. Gives three steams of Church history—Catholic, Protestant, and the *persecuted remnant.*

The Unshakable Kingdom and the Unchanging Person. Jones, E. Stanley. Abingdon Press, Nashville, TN, 1972. Now available through Life Changes, P.O. Box 98088, Raleigh, NC 27624. How the church should impact all of society.

The Use of Houses in Early Christianity. Jones, Jerry. Boston Church of Christ, Box 144, Lexington, MA 02173, 1984. On the subject of house churches.

The Way Church Ought to Be. Lund, Robert A. Outside the Box Press, P.O. Box 151, Albany, OR 97321, 2001. Very radical and quite thorough, 464 pages.

Thoughts on Christian Fellowship. Lindell, John. 8783 Northwood Road, Everson, WA 98247, 1964. How to experience true *koinonia.*

Toward a House Church Theology. Atkerson, Steve, ed. New Testament Restoration Foundation, 2752 Evans Dale Circle, Atlanta, GA 30340, 1996.

Where Do We Go From Here? Neighbour, Ralph W. Touch Publications, P.O. Box 19888, Houston, TX 77224, 1990. A guidebook for cell-group churches.

Who is Your Covering? A Fresh Look at Leadership, Authority and Accountability. Viola, Frank. Present Testimony Ministry, 918 Delaney Circle #205, Brandon, FL 33511. How leadership, authority, and accountability functioned in the early church. It takes dead aim at the abuses of authority that mark many modern churches and sheds fresh light on how to secure Christ's Headship in His Body today.

Will the Real Heretics Please Stand Up. Bercot, David W. Scroll Publishing Company, P.O. Box 6175, Tyler, TX 75711, 1989. A comparison of today's Christianity with the radical Christianity of the early Church.

WOMAN–God's Plan, not Man's Tradition. Krupp, Joanne. Preparing the Way Publishers, 2121 Barnes Avenue SE, Salem, OR 97306. Excellent on God's plan for women.

Women Elders: Sinners or Servants? Kroeger, Richard & Catherine. Christians for Biblical Equality, 380 Lafayette Freeway #122, St. Paul, MN 55107. The possibility of women elders as seen in the New Testament.

Additional Helps

You may find these to be of help on an on-going basis.

Christian Leadership University

The purpose of Christian Leadership University is to raise up leaders in every discipline of life who can creatively integrate biblical principles with the Holy Spirit's anointing. Since study is done in your home at your own pace, you can design your own study program and be in touch with your instructors via email, faxes, and the telephone. Both undergraduate and graduate degrees are available in the Colleges of Communication, Creativity, Education, Human Services, and Leadership. CLU is accredited by the World-Wide Accreditation Commission of Christian Educational Institutions (WWAC) and certified by the Apostolic Council for Educational Accountability (ACEA). A Certificate in Christian Ministry is available for courses designed and taught by Nate Krupp. These courses include New Testament Survey, How to Study the Bible, Personal Evangelism, Qualities GOD is Looking for in Us, What GOD is Saying to the Church Today, Foundational Studies About the Christian Faith, GOD's Release of Women, Getting to Know GOD, House Church,

Leadership-Servanthood in the Church, and others.

House 2 House Magazine

House 2 House magazine has been established to help house churches across a broad spectrum of theological and practical expressions. This free subscription magazine is now going out to more than 20,000 people nationwide every other month, and in the process, is challenging all house churches to keep an outward focus alongside an inner deepening of the local church's devotion to the Lord and ability to follow the leading of the Holy Spirit. To subscribe, go online to www.house2house.tv or call their office at 512-282-2322.

Web Sites – Discussion Lists

http://www.home-church.org The HCDL (Home Church Discussion List) was established in 1995 to foster communication among Christians involved in home churches.

http://housechurch.org/talk HCTalk (House Church Talk) is an email discussion list concerning all matters house church, with an emphasis on the person and work of our Lord Jesus Christ.

http://world-missions.org/planting NTCP (New Testament Church Planting) is an email list which emphasizes church multiplication through mutual ministry and house to house meetings.

Web Sites – Locating House Churches

There are several directories for finding a home church group in your geographic area:
www.hccentral.com/directory
www.homechurch.com
www.housechurch.org/registry
www.house2house.tv

Other Helpful Web Sites

You will find other helpful connections by checking out the links listed on our web sites at:
www.radchr.net
ptwpublish.com

Additional Books from PTWP

These books from PTWP will help you discover God's plan for His Church.

The Church Triumphant at the End of the Age

Nate Krupp. The end-time Church characterized by revival, restoration, unity, world evangelization, and persecution. Also traces revival, restoration, and world evangelization throughout Church history. A major work. 360 pages • $12.95

New Wine Skins – The Church in Transition

Nate Krupp. Fifteen ways that God is changing His Church today to get ready for coming revival, harvest, and persecution.
ISBN 1-929451-14-8 • 32 pages • $4 or 3 for $10

WOMAN–God's Plan, not Man's Tradition

Joanne Krupp. This book examines every major passage in the Bible on the subject of God's plan for women. It refutes the traditional teachiing of husbands having authority over their wives and of a limited role for women in the Church. It biblically releases women to become all that God intends them to be as equal partners in the home and the Church. The conclusions of this book need to be prayerfully considered by all—men and women!
ISBN 1-929451-00-8 • 154 pages • $11.95

Leadership-Servanthood in the Church

Nate Krupp. A book which examines every major passage in the New Testament on the subject of leadership. You may be surprised at some of the findings.
ISBN 1-929451-15-6 • 22 pages • $5

The Church in the House – A Return to Simplicity

Robert Fitts, Sr. This is another classic on the subject of home church. Evangelize the world quickly by planting millions of house churches everywhere. This book tells you how. Earlier editions of this book have already gone around the world. We are thrilled to be able to publish this new, revised edition.
ISBN 1-929451-07-5 • 116 pages • $9.95

Restoring the Vision of the End-times Church

Vern Kuenzi. This is no typical book on how to improve the church. This is a very strong word to the Body of Christ on what's ahead for God's people. As a theological-biblical treatise it is the best exposition this author has seen on the subject of the Church and end-times. But it is more than that. It is a major prophetic word to the Church about her future—a warning that days of persecution and suffering are ahead. But that persecution and suffering is set in the context of God's glory and eternal purpose, and a Church with great purity, authority, power, and anointing.
ISBN 1-929451-01-6 • 252 pages • $15.95

These books from PTWP will take you deeper in your relationship with God.

Knowing GOD Series

This series consists of five study books. Each one takes you deeper in your knowledge of God's Word and in your relationship with Him. You do not need to do the series in the given order (1-5), but you may find that helpful.

#1 Basic Bible Studies
ISBN 1-929451-02-4 • 80 pages $11.95
A question-and-answer type, foundational Bible study book about the Christian faith. Chapters include:

1. Is There a God?
2. The Issue of Sin
3. What Provision Did God Make for Man's Sin?
4. How Should Man Respond to God's Provision?
5. Abiding in Christ
6. The Christian and God's Word
7. The Christian and Prayer
8. The Christian and the Holy Spirit
9. The Christian and Warfare
10. The Christian and Witnessing
11. The Christian and the Home
12. The Christian and the Church
13. The Christian and Business Affairs
14. The Christian and Discipleship
15. The Christian and Service
16. The Christian and the Return of Christ

#2 New Testament Survey Course
ISBN 1-929451-03-2 • 234 pages $16.95
This is a very unique 47-lesson Bible study survey of the New Testament.

- It covers every verse of the New Testament
- It leads you in an in-depth study of each book. You will read the entire New Testament and either answer summarizing questions or summarize the book, a paragraph at a time.

- It harmonizes the Gospels so that you study Jesus' life in a single, chronological narrative.
- It places the letters in the order in which they were actually written.
- This study gives you background information on each book of the New Testament.
- You will apply each book to your own life situation.
- You will decide on verses to memorize from each book.
- You will know the New Testament when you have finished this study!

#3 **Mastering the Word of God - and Letting It Master You!**
ISBN 1-929451-04-0 • 46 pages $6.95
Workbook • ISBN 1-929451-09-1 • 34 pgs . . $5.95
This book is about various methods of in-depth Bible intake: how to hear, read, study, memorize, and meditate on the Word of God. With this book you will learn how to study the Bible. You will be able to develop a life-long plan of in-depth Bible study - mastering God's Word, and letting It master you.
Bible Outlines
ISBN 1-929451-10-5 • 62 pgs $9.95
A supplemental book to Mastering the Word of God.
This book gives an outline for every book of the Bible, a title for every chapter, and other helpful information.

#4 **Getting to Know GOD**
ISBN 1-929451-05-9 • 288 pages $19.95
A devotional Bible study book on 57 aspects of GOD's Person, Character, and Attributes: His love, His mercy, His faithfulness, His goodness, His glory and majesty, etc. For each attribute, you will read an introduction, prayerfully read three or four pages of appropriate

Scripture verses, answer study questions, do research, meditate on and apply the lesson to your life, memorize verses of your choice, and pray a closing prayer. This book was written by an actual Bible study group. This study will change your life!

#5 Qualities God is Looking for in Us
ISBN 1-929451-06-7 • 384 pages $24.95

A 53-week Bible study, devotional book on the qualities God is looking for in us: abiding in Christ, boldness, contentment, diligence, discipline, early riser, forgiving, generous, holy, honest, humble, obedient, praiser, prayer, servant, wise, zealous, etc. For each quality, you will read an introduction, prayerfully read three or four pages of appropriate Scripture verses, answer study questions, do research, meditate on and apply the lesson to your life, memorize verses of your choice, and pray a closing prayer. This book was written by an actual Bible Study group. This study will greatly challenge you!

Other Books from PTWP

Foundations for the Christian Life by John G. Gill. This 118-page book is written to give the foundation stones for the Christian life, as listed in Hebrews 6:1-3. Many Christians struggle in their Christian life because the proper foundation was not laid in the beginning. This book biblically gives this proper foundation. Questions at the end of each chapter make it even more practical.
ISBN 1-929451-11-3 • $11.95

Fulfilling the Great Commission by A.D. 2000 and Beyond by Nate Krupp. A 12-page booklet on the need—and what it will take—to evangelize the world. Very important! $1.00

God's Word Puts the Wind in My Sails by Joanne Bachran. A guide to knowing GOD and His Word. It is full of helpful, basic material for all believers, especially new Christians. A reference guide, Bible study, personal devotional, and journal—all rolled into one. A personal compass for a more intimate relationship with God. Very useful!
ISBN 1-929451-08-3 • 216 pages • $13.95

Mobilizing Prayer for World Evangelization by Nate Krupp. A 32-page, basic, study booklet on prayer. Has been used in prayer seminars and retreats throughout the United States. $2.00

The Way to God. A 16-page witnessing booklet you can use to lead your unsaved friends to Jesus. It has been used around the world, on every continent. People have been saved just by reading it. Includes the biblical emphases of repentance and the Lordship of Jesus Christ. $.25 ea., 10 for $2, 100 for $15

You Can Be a Soul Winner—Here's How! by Nate Krupp. A 176-page book of practical, personal evangelism know-how. Has been used on every continent. Over 55,000 copies in print. $11.95

ORDER FORM

Preparing the Way Publishers

2121 Barnes Avenue SE, Salem, OR 97306, USA

Voice 503-585-4054 • Fax 503-375-8401

E-mail: kruppnj@open.org • Website: www.PTWpublish.com

BOOKS ABOUT THE CHURCH

QTY	TITLE	PRICE	TOTAL
_____	Leadership—Servanthood in the Church $5.00	_____
_____	New Wine Skins—the Church in Transition . . .$4.00, 3 for $10.00	_____
_____	Restoring the Vision of the End-times Church $15.95	_____
_____	The Church in the House $9.95	_____
_____	The Church Triumphant $12.95	_____
_____	Woman—God's Plan Not Man's Tradition $11.95	_____

KNOWING GOD SERIES

_____	#1 Basic Bible Studies $11.95	_____
_____	#2 New Testament Survey Course $16.95	_____
_____	#3 Mastering the Word of God $6.95	_____
_____	Workbook $5.95	_____
_____	Bible Outlines $9.95	_____
_____	#4 Getting to Know GOD $19.95	_____
_____	#5 Qualities GOD is Looking for in Us $24.95	_____

OTHER BOOKS

_____	Foundations for the Christian Life $11.95	_____
_____	Fulfilling the Great Commission by A.D. 2000 and Beyond . . .$1.00	_____
_____	God's Word Puts the Wind in My Sail $13.95	_____
_____	Mobilizing Prayer for World Evangelization $2.00	_____
_____	The Way to God . . . . .25¢ ea., 10 for $2.00, 100 for $15.00	_____
_____	You Can Be a Soul Winner—Here's How $11.95	_____

Ordering Information: Fill in your order and send it **with payment** to Preparing the Way Publishers for processing. A new copy of this Order Form will be included with your order for your future ordering use.

Payments: To avoid extra bookkeeping and handling expenses, credits for less than $1.00 will not be sent. Prices are subject to change without notice. **Full payment is expected with order.**

Postage and Handling for mainland United States orders:

Amount of Order	P & H	Postage and Handling for Alaska, Hawaii,
Under $20.00	$4.00	U.S. possessions, and all other nations:
$20.00 - $39.99	15%	Actual postage charge plus 10% handling
$40.00 and above	10%	

TOTAL Book Order $ _____

Plus Postage & Handling $ _____

GRAND TOTAL $ _____

Ship To:

Name: _____ Date of Order: _____

Address: _____ Telephone: _____

City _____ State _____ Zip_____ Nation _____

Clip and mail

Printed in the United States
34735LVS00002B/241